The publisher gratefully acknowledges the generous
support of the Ahmanson Foundation Humanities
Endowment Fund of the University of California Press
Foundation.

In Search of a
Concrete Music

In Search of a
Concrete Music

PIERRE SCHAEFFER

Translated by Christine North and John Dack

UNIVERSITY OF CALIFORNIA PRESS
Berkeley   Los Angeles   London

University of California Press, one of the most distinguished university presses in the United States, enriches lives around the world by advancing scholarship in the humanities, social sciences, and natural sciences. Its activities are supported by the UC Press Foundation and by philanthropic contributions from individuals and institutions. For more information, visit www.ucpress.edu.

University of California Press
Berkeley and Los Angeles, California

University of California Press, Ltd.
London, England

Library of Congress Cataloging-in-Publication Data

Schaeffer, Pierre, 1910–1995, author.
 [A la recherche d'une musique concrète. English]
 In search of a concrete music / Pierre Schaeffer ; translated by Christine North and John Dack.
    pages   cm. — (California studies in 20th-century music ; 15)
 Originally published: A la recherche d'une musique concrète / Pierre Schaeffer. Paris : Éditions du Seuil, 1952.
 Includes bibliographical references and index.
 ISBN 978-0-520-26573-8 (cloth : alk. paper) — ISBN 978-0-520-26574-5 (pbk. : alk. paper)
 1. Musique concrète—History and criticism.   I. North, Christine, translator.   II. Dack, John, translator.   III. Title.
 ML3817.S2613   2012
 786.7′ 5—dc23

                                                    2012029627

Originally published as *A la recherche d'une musique concrète* by Pierre Schaeffer, © Editions du Seuil, 1952.

22   21   20   19   18   17   16   15   14   13
10   9   8   7   6   5   4   3   2   1

Contents

Illustrations

Captions enclosed in brackets beneath the figures in the text have been supplied from the following list, which was included at the end of the French edition; those figures did not have captions in the original text.

Translators' Note

Pierre Schaeffer was indisputably a polymath. He described himself as an *écrivain,* and the range of his writings, which included not only fiction (the novel *Clotaire Nicole*) but also articles, essays, and books, many devoted to the increasing cultural significance of the broadcasting media, is impressive. An *écrivain,* therefore, he certainly was. But Schaeffer was also a broadcaster, composer, and music theorist. These activities are all the more remarkable if we consider the onerous nature of his duties as an administrator at the Radiodiffusion-Télévision Française (RTF)—which later became the Office de Radiodiffusion-Télévision Française, or ORTF—and the distraction of time-consuming visits to former French colonies, where he helped to establish radio stations.

However, a polymath's productivity can engender suspicion as well as admiration, and an accurate assessment of such a diverse body of work becomes problematic. Such an undertaking is particularly challenging in Great Britain, where, regrettably, intellectuals are frequently treated with mistrust—foreign ones even more so. Schaeffer's achievements are acknowledged in books published in English on the history of electronic music, though they rarely situate his complex and subtle theoretical system within the broader sweep of the history of ideas. He is characterized as a radio engineer who developed an interesting, if somewhat idiosyncratic, method of composing music and investigating potential musical material by means of the technology of the radio station.

This is, broadly speaking, concrete music, and for most musicians it is Schaeffer's principal achievement. Indeed, his technique of manipulating recordings of real-world sounds is regarded as prescient. Not only the physical methods of studio practice but also the actual recorded materials are relevant to contemporary musicians in both technologically mediated composition and performance (though now the technology is overwhelmingly digital rather than analogue). Nevertheless, such accounts appear to be unacquainted with Schaeffer's formidable training as a radio engineer, his awareness of traditional musical skills, his emphasis on the listener's perceptual activity, and his profound knowledge of French literature and thought, particularly that of the post-Romantic era. And yet these are precisely what enabled him to explore in his own inimitable manner the relationship between broadcasting media and sound-based art forms—principally music.

Our intention is not to criticize these books on music history and technology. There has been a marked improvement in Schaeffer studies since the 1990s, and concrete music is no longer regarded as a colorful if rather inconsequential prelude to the more important activities of the Nordwestdeutscher Rundfunk (NWDR) studio in Cologne.

A la recherche d'une musique concrète contains the first hints of Schaeffer's sophisticated attitude regarding the effects of technology on the processes of composition and listening. Schaeffer frequently used the term *généraliser*, and it is important to remember that his ideas, particularly in later works such as the *Traité des objets musicaux* (1966), can be applied beyond their obvious origins of studio practice. For example, analyses of the status and role of the musical instrument (always a contentious issue in contemporary technological contexts) benefit from Schaeffer's insights. Moreover, his concern with sound classification and description transcended physical causality and has consequences for evaluating how any sound might function at any structural level. Our description of him as, among other things, a "music theorist" is thus deliberate, though it is a music theory grounded in (although not limited to) studio practices of the immediate postwar period. Schaeffer's reputation in France is assured. The saying "A prophet hath no honor in his own country" (John 4:44) cannot be applied to Schaeffer. We believe the disparity between French opinion and that of the Anglophone community is largely due to the inaccessibility of Schaeffer's texts to those with a limited command of French. We thus believe that this translation of one of Pierre Schaeffer's seminal texts is urgently needed not only for its own intrinsic interest, but also for the contribution it can make to the reevaluation of this talented visionary.

From the translator's point of view, it is important to keep in mind Schaeffer's wit and self-deprecating humor, his readiness to criticize his own as well as others' ideas, and his love of language and literature, which can be seen in his playful or dry turns of phrase and his many indirect and direct references to other writers as well as mythological and biblical sources. The title of the work itself is a clear reference to Marcel Proust's famous sequence of novels, *A la recherche du temps perdu (In Search of Lost Time)*. We have endeavored throughout to translate the text into academic English of the 1950s, with which we are familiar and which has many of the same features as Schaeffer's French. At the same time, keeping in mind that much of the work is in diary form, we have used more relaxed contractions and expressions where appropriate. A trend in modern translation is to produce a version—almost a revision of the original text—in a modern, accessible idiom, which purportedly communicates the work's essential meaning but also foregrounds the translator as an active creator in his or her own right. The drawbacks of such an approach, particularly in the case of academic works, are obvious: the translator's interpretation can only be one of many, and the modern idiom can become just as dated, if not more so, than the original, giving the reader an added level of interpretation to deal with. Although, of course, it is impossible for translators not to leave any stamp at all on a text, we have tried to be as faithful as possible to the original in order to give the reader, as nearly as we can, the experience of actually reading Schaeffer.

One of the problems arising from this approach is the noninclusive nature of Schaeffer's language, which was, of course, quite standard in his day. After much thought, we decided not to change the basically male-centered style, and we have left all pronouns in the masculine and referred to people in general as "men." We hope that readers will accept this characteristic as giving a sense of period to the text. However, where references to other cultures and peoples were concerned, we felt that Schaeffer's lack of what is now called "political correctness" might give real offense, and so we have changed expressions such as *"le tam-tam nègre," "nègre," "peaux-rouges,"* and *"Hottentot"* to terms we hope will be more acceptable to a modern reader (in these cases, "native tom-tom," "black," "Native American," and "native South African").

Another problem for any translator of an academic work in French is that the language is relatively abstract and theoretical compared to English; one might even say that the mode of thinking itself tends to be more schematic, with a readiness to see material for study in terms of highly abstract dualisms and correlations, which on occasion does not sit easily with the perhaps more pragmatic English language. This creates several problems of translation affecting key terms. Perhaps the most obvious of these is the word *concret/concrète* itself. The word in French, which has nothing of the familiar meaning of "concrete" in English, is used throughout the text with all its usual French connotations of "palpable," "nontheoretical," and "experiential," all of which pertain to a greater or lesser extent to the type of music Schaeffer is pioneering. Despite the risk of ambiguity, we decided to translate it with the English word *concrete* in most contexts, as an expression such as "real-world" does not cover the original's range of meanings, and in particular it would not link with the main subject of the book. In some cases, to avoid obvious or rather comical ambiguity, we have used quotation marks or changed the phrasing, using, for example, "concrete" musicians or "composers of concrete music" rather than "concrete musicians" or "concrete composers." Where the official title of experimental music and the group founded by Schaeffer are concerned, we have retained his own term, "Musique Concrète," which he later claims to have coined. Until this point (and in the title of the work), where Schaeffer is referring only to a possible "concrete music," we have translated the expression into English.

A further key concept underpinning much of this book is contained in the contrasted terms *sujet/objet* (subject/object): in Schaeffer's writing, *"sujet"* denotes the individual person, the subjective "I," and *"objet"* the external-world object of his or her attention or study, where English would tend to use "subject," as in "the subject of my thesis." To avoid confusion, we have retained Schaeffer's scrupulous distinction.

Another word that causes particular problems in this book is *expéri-ence*, which denotes both "experiment" and "experience" in English. There are several instances in which it is almost impossible to know whether Schaeffer meant one, the other, or both, and indeed it is not clear whether the French mind makes this distinction at all. In some cases the ambiguity remains unresolved and the word retains elements of both "experiment" and "experience." Perhaps the most obvious example is the title of the third section, which we have translated as "The Concrete Experiment in Music," but which also suggests "The Concrete Experience." In this and many other examples, we would ask the reader to keep something of both meanings in mind.

This book introduces one of the many terms Schaeffer was to stamp with his own particular meaning, the word *allure*, which in French con-notes "way of walking," extending into "speed of movement," "bearing." In this early work Schaeffer uses "allure" to describe the way that sound moves over time (see figs. 28, 36), but in his *Traité des objets musicaux* (Trea-tise on musical objects) he describes it as "more or less regular oscilla-tions." To translate "allure" as "gait," perhaps the most accurate English equivalent, would both risk confusion with its homophone "gate" and miss Schaeffer's specific meaning. Words such as "movement," however seem too general. We have therefore decided to retain the French word despite its different meaning in English.

ACKNOWLEDGMENTS

We should like to thank above all Madame Jacqueline Schaeffer. This translation would not have been possible without her tireless support and constant encouragement. She has also given us invaluable practical help, not only in the provision of the photograph on the front cover of this book, but also by helping us through her own personal experience to understand Pierre Schaeffer's personality and intentions. Our thanks also go to Professor Martin Laliberté of the Université de Paris-Est Marne-la-Vallée for his many indispensable insights and suggestions along the way. Furthermore, we are extremely grateful to Peter Williams of Middlesex University for producing the diagrams. In conclusion, we should, of course, like to express our gratitude to all the staff at the University of California Press who have guided and assisted us at all stages of this complex project. One final word of sincere thanks is due to Douglas Kahn, who first suggested that we undertake this translation.

MAY,

FOR ONCE,

THE ADMINISTRATION

OF FRENCH RADIO AND TELEVISION AS A

LEGAL PERSONA

RECEIVE IN DEDICATION AS DID

THE PRINCE

THE HOMAGE OF WORK ACCOMPLISHED

WITHOUT FORGETTING THE PHYSICAL PERSONA

OF ITS DIRECTOR GENERAL

MONSIEUR WLADIMIR PORCHÉ

WHO WAS KIND ENOUGH TO PROVIDE

RESEARCH INTO CONCRETE MUSIC

WITH THE RAREST OF THE FAVORS OF POWER:

CONTINUITY

First Journal
of Concrete Music

1948–1949

1

Need for the implicit. From the ski tow to the noise piano.
Wherein the autodidact feels guilty. Wherein chance neverthe-
less comes to his aid. On the merit of accepting evidence, after
denying it. That it is no longer the same. That the most general
musical instrument possible is not inconceivable.

1948. January. Sometimes when I write I am envious of more intense modes of expression. Writing is always making explicit at the expense of other things. Mystery is sacrificed, and consequently truth and so everything. At these moments I am overwhelmed by a longing for music that, as Roger Ducasse says, "he likes because it does not mean anything."

February. The change of scenery makes me forget the weight on my mind. Without memories, without worries, I can feel stirrings deep within me. Ideas are seeking outlets other than words: Ta ra ra ra boom—whistlings—the snow—gusts of perfect fullness of sound—no will to conclude. On the windswept plateau, right at the top of the ski tow, iron hooks turn around the wheel, having scraped the frozen snow away. The whirligig of this mechanism injures the frost-crystal. Yet these things must, of necessity, be in harmony. A heterogeneous universe torments us. People today return to nature in bouts of ski tows, half-tracks, Kandahar ropes, super-light alloys. Thus, perfectly equipped, chrome-shod, asbestos-gloved, nylon-clad, they sample the immaculate mountain air. They are caught between two fires that burn and freeze them simultaneously. I must find a way to express this.

March. Back in Paris I have started to collect objects. I have a "Symphony of noises" in mind; after all, there has been a symphony of psalms. I go to the sound effects department of the French radio service. I find clappers, coconut shells, klaxons, bicycle horns. I imagine a scale of bicycle horns. There are gongs and birdcalls. It is charming that an administrative system should be concerned with birdcalls and should regularize their acquisition on an official form, duly recorded.

I take away doorbells, a set of bells, an alarm clock, two rattles, two childishly painted whirligigs. The clerk causes some difficulties. Usually, he is asked for a particular item. There are no sound effects without a text in parallel, are there? But what about the person who wants noise without text or context?

To tell the truth, I suspect that none of these objects will be of any use to me. They are too explicit. Some wrangles with the Administration and, not without signing several authorizations, I take them away.

I take them with the joy of a child coming out of the loft with his arms full of embarrassing, albeit useless, things and not without a powerful sense of my ridiculousness, guilt even.

April 1. We shall better understand the unease of the concrete musician if we compare his intentions and his means. This, for example, is what we find in his notes:

> On a rhythmic ostinato, occasionally interrupted by a logarithmic rallentando, superimposition of circular noises; cadence of pure noises (?). Then fugue of differential noises. Conclude with a series of beatings with alternating slack and tight sounds. The whole thing to be treated as an andante. Don't be afraid of length, or slowness.

April 3. The objects are now put away in a cupboard in the Studio d'Essai (Experimental Studio). I need a metronome. The one that was sent to me does not beat in time, nor do the ones that followed. It is incredible how much a metronome can lack a sense of rhythm!

April 4. Sudden illumination. Add a component of sound to noise, that is, combine a melodic element with the percussive element. From this, the notion of wood cut into different lengths, of approximately tuned tubes. First attempts.

April 5. My bits of wood are pathetic. I need a workshop. It's already bad enough trying to cut them to different lengths and from various materials. Afterward, they have to be arranged so that they can be played easily. I'm up against the problem of the piano again. By "noise piano" I mean the pile of materials that are crammed into the studio. Regular visitors to the Studio d'Essai, who are no longer surprised by my eccentricities, now think I am a nuisance. I have been coveting the workbench in the workshop for a week. I'm asking for it to be moved out. It's sturdy and doesn't vibrate. I can nail all sorts of supports to it. I arrange my little bells and a row of bicycle horns on it.

I'm still not sure about these preparations.

April 7. Second illumination. All these clumsy bits of wood constitute a lesson in things; they are nothing other than resonators tuned to half wavelengths: they are fixed at a "node," and an "antinode" vibrates at their free end. My truancy comes to a sudden end; I am led back into the classroom: first lesson in acoustics and music theory. The Conservatory and the Faculty give me a poor mark.

Let us take the experiment as far as it will go. I need organ parts, not "a noise-piano." I go to Cavaillé-Coll and Pleyel. There I find parts of an organ destroyed in the bombing. I return with a truckload of "thirty-two footers" and tongued reeds. My originality will be not to play them like an organist but to hit them with a mallet, detune them perhaps. The war had already taken this on.

April 12. I need some helpers for my increasingly laborious trials. One of them blows into the two largest pipes, which are pleasantly only a "small tone" apart. (We laugh a lot at this expression, small tone or large semitone—as you please.) The second helper, armed with two mallets, covers with great difficulty an octave of xylophonic recumbent effigies. A third is in charge of the little bells. I compose a score of several bars. We rehearse, make mistakes, begin again, record. The result is woeful.

While the sound produced by the large square wooden pipe is curious, varying (according to whether it is struck at different places, on different supports), the score is pathetically inadequate. I now feel as if I'm going backward. I can hardly tolerate the deference that surrounds me. What do they want from me and these trials when I am so deeply convinced that I'm going down a blind alley?

April 15. I retain only two or three curios from these trials: a vibrating metal strip that you can bring into contact with any object. It then produces a "knocking noise." Dampen the vibration of a crystal glass, a bell, with your fingernail, or cardboard, or a piece of metal, and you mingle noise, sound, a rhythm.

Conversely, I am trying to construct an automatically vibrating metal strip (like a doorbell) that I can bring into contact with various sound bodies. In this way I get a mode of attack from these bodies, which superimposes the noise and rhythm of the attack on the sound. The results are profoundly monotonous.

Furthermore, all these noises are identifiable. As soon as you hear them, they suggest glass, a bell, wood, a gong, iron . . . I'm giving up on music.

April 18. You can't be in two places at once. I must choose between the Studio and the sound booth. This is where I finally took refuge. A window protects me from the Studio. I am among the turntables, the mixer, the potentiometers. I feel vaguely reassured. I operate through intermediaries. I no longer manipulate sound objects myself. I listen to their effect through the microphone. Which amounts to burying my head in the sand, since the microphone only gives the raw sound with some secondary effects and qualitatively adds nothing. However, the sense of security that I feel in the sound booth gives me strength to continue these experiments for some days more, even though I now expect nothing from them.

April 19. By having one of the bells hit I got the sound *after* the attack. Without its percussion the bell becomes an oboe sound. I prick up my ears. Has a breach appeared in the enemy ranks? Has the advantage changed sides?

April 21. If I cut off the sounds from their attacks, I get a different sound; on the other hand, if I compensate for the drop in intensity with the potentiometer, I get a drawn-out sound and can move the continuation at will. So I record a series of notes made in this way, each one on a disc. By arranging the discs on record players, I can, using the controls, play these notes as I wish, one after the other or simultaneously. Of course, the manipulation is unwieldy, unsuited to any virtuosity; but I have a musical instrument. A new instrument? I am doubtful. I am wary of new instruments, ondes or ondiolines, what the Germans pompously call *"elektronische Musik."* When I encounter any electronic music I react like my violinist father, or my mother, a singer. We are craftsmen. In all this wooden and tin junk and in my bicycle horns I rediscover my violin, my voice. I am seeking direct contact with sound material, without any electrons getting in the way.

April 22. Once my initial joy is past, I ponder. I've already got quite a lot of problems with my turntables because there is only one note per turntable. With a cinematographic flash-forward, Hollywood style, I see myself surrounded by twelve dozen turntables, each with one note. Yet it would be, as mathematicians would say, the *most general musical instrument possible.*

   Is it another blind alley, or am I in possession of a solution whose importance I can only guess at?

April 23. This time I am thinking in the abstract: science and hypothesis . . . Say, an organ with each key linked to a turntable that would have appropriate discs put on it as required; let's suppose that the keyboard of this organ switches on the record players simultaneously or one after the other, at the moment and for the length of time desired, by means of a mixer switch with "n" commands; *in theory* we get a mother instrument, capable of replacing not only all existing instruments but every conceivable instrument, musical or not, whether or not their notes are at given pitches in the tessitura. For the moment, this instrument is entirely in my imagination, but, to a certain extent, it can be realized. In any case, as, for practical and economic reasons, it cannot be realized soon, it can act as a working hypothesis, the framework for a theory. What a blessing a scientific education is! Without means of experimentation you are allowed, for a time, to carry on with the experiment purely through the imagination. So for a time I am playing this *most general piano possible* in my mind—an instrument for encyclopedists. Isn't this the century for a new encyclopedia?

End of April. I spend these days in a state of half belief. If you invent, you must get a patent. A half smile: can you patent an idea? It seems you can.

I experiment tirelessly. It is surprising to note how *the same process* carried out endlessly and in different ways never entirely exhausts reality: there is always more to be learned, and always some unexpected outcome takes us by surprise. For the principle is everything.

I shall go over what has happened.

Where does the invention come from? When did it occur? I reply unhesitatingly: when I *interfered with* the sound of the bells. Separating the sound from the attack was the generative act. The whole of concrete music was contained in embryo in this inherently creative act with sound material. I have no particular memory of the moment when I made this recording. At first the discovery remained unnoticed. I give thanks for my stubbornness. When you persist against all logic, it's because you're expecting something from a chance event that logic couldn't have foreseen. My merit is that I noticed the one experiment among a hundred, apparently just as disappointing as the others, which provided a way out. I also needed the boldness to generalize.

Besides, very often we don't get anything from revelations that come from experimental accident. Here is an example: everyone has played sound backward. It's a strange phenomenon, and we sometimes get surprising effects from it. But, as far as I know, no one has ever drawn *general* conclusions. No one has ever considered sound played backward as musical material that can be constructed and structured. Yet sound played backward already doubles, at least a priori, the number of known instruments. The musical community doesn't care; however, for twenty years the experiment has been taking place every day.

Of course, the experiment only pays off if it gives rise immediately to experimentation: piano chords played backward are only interesting subject to certain conditions. Then you can get organ sounds, or peals of bells from the piano. The instrumentalist is then no longer the winner of the Prix du Conservatoire but the sound engineer.

2

On the use of the railway engine as an orchestral instrument.
Diabolus in Mecanica. The whole art is in hearing. The sound
object in itself. Definition of concrete music. Wherein quantity
becomes quality. The diapason concertino. L'Etude aux
tourniquets (Whirligig study). L'Etude violette (Purple study)
and l'Etude noire (Black study). L'Etude no. 5, the "saucepan"
study.

Easter. Two days in the country banish my enthusiasm for the most-general-possible piano. I realize that I have made scarcely any progress in my plan to express something with noises. I've experimented for two months and composed nothing. All I've discovered is a tool. A tool—isn't that something? No, in this age of productivity, and for the busy people that we are. How can I justify time spent (more than two months without results . . . concrete ones), records wasted (about a hundred already)? And then, experimenting is all very fine, but self-expression is so tempting!

So I'm already turning my back on fortune and departing from the narrow—and thus the longest and the most tortuous—way; I am, quite wrongly, looking for a shortcut.

Certainly the idea of a concert of railway engines is exciting. Sensational. Too much so. I've already forgotten the failure of my organ pipes.

Why should whistles, just because they come from boilers, be more interesting? But once again I have to learn from experience.

May 3. So here I am on my way to Batignolles station, escorted by a mobile sound unit and naïvely cherishing my wrongheaded bright idea.

Six engines at the depot, taken by surprise, as it were, at home. I ask the drivers to improvise. One to start, the others to reply. These engines do certainly have voices of their own. One is hoarse, another harsh; one has a deep voice, another a strident one. I eagerly record the dialogue between these mild-mannered whales. At their conductors' desks the Batignolles drivers watch me but quickly grow tired. You can sense that engines can't like being performers. What a divide there was between my momentary infatuation—this instant when, in the cold light of day, the recording vouchsafes me a panting, feeble conversation entirely lacking in rhythm!

I should have liked precise variations: the noise of the engine with its wheels spinning downhill, its rapid panting echoing back into the distance, the clash of buffers and their delicate ornamentation, the hammer blow, with that long-handled hammer that they use to tap the bogies . . . I'm a bit disappointed: no wheels spinning downhill, the leisurely puffing of a solo engine. A tiny, gentle touching of buffers, with neither semiquaver nor grace notes. It's a good job the record library has a large selection of sounds of coaches going along railway lines.

May 5. Further irresolvable difficulties. I have composed a score. Eight bars getting under way. Accelerando by solo locomotive, then tutti of coaches. Rhythms. Some are very fine. I have isolated a certain number of leitmotifs that I must make into transitions and counterpoint. Then slow down and stop. A cadence of buffer clashes. Da capo and reprise, more energetically, of the preceding elements. Crescendo. Effect of trains passing each other in opposite directions with that inflection when moving things pass each other and their sound goes down one tone, an augmented second, sometimes a third. But truly it's difficult not to be led by these records. How can I compose them if I reject the idea of a dramatic scenario?

As soon as a record is put on the turntable a magic power enchains me, forces me to submit to it, however, monotonous it is. Do we give ourselves over because we are in on the act? Why shouldn't they broadcast three minutes of "pure coach" telling people that they only need to know how to listen, and that the whole art is in hearing? Because they are extraordinary to listen to, provided you have reached that special state of mind that I'm now in. How much I prefer them in their raw state, rather than in the state of vague composition (decomposition) where I have finally, and with great difficulty, isolated eight pseudobars in one pseudorhythm . . .

I lower the pickup arm as one rhythmic group starts. I raise it just as it ends, I link it with another, and so on. How powerful our imagination is! When in our minds we pick out a certain rhythmic or melodic outline in a sound fragment like this, we think we have its musical element. We link things together, we contrast, we superimpose them. We even attempt to write down notes. We are momentarily filled with enthusiasm. In reality, when we listen again, impartially, to what we have composed, obtained after long hours of patience, all we find is a crude concatenation of rhythmic groups resistant to any regular rhythm. I imagined I had extracted a three-four, a six-eight from the moving coach. The train beats its own time, perfectly clear but perfectly irrational. The most monotonous of trains has constant variations of rhythm. It never plays in time. It changes into a series of isotopes.

But then, what subtle musical pleasure a practiced ear could find learning to listen to, to play this new-style Czerny! Then, without the help of any melody, any harmony, you would only need to be able to discern and savor, in the most mechanistic monotony, the interplay of a few atoms of freedom, the imperceptible improvisations of chance . . .

May 7. I'm spending two sessions on the noise of buffers. I've finally got some quite good ones, particularly if I set them up on the double turntable to echo each other. I try a sort of canon. They answer each other pianissimo, then sforzando. It's exciting, but is it music? Isn't the noise of buffers first and foremost anecdotal, and thus antimusical? If this is so, then there's no hope and my research is absurd.

May 10. My composition hesitates between two options: dramatic or musical sequences.

The dramatic sequence constrains the imagination. We witness events; departures, stops. We observe. The engine moves, the track is empty or not. The machine toils, pants, relaxes—anthropomorphism. All of this is the opposite of music. However, I've managed to isolate a rhythm and contrast it with itself in a different sound *color*. Dark, light, dark, light. This rhythm could very well remain unchanged for a long time. It creates a sort of identity for itself, and repeating it makes you forget it's a train.

Is this a sequence that can be called musical? If I extract any sound element and repeat it without bothering about its *form* but varying its *matter*, I practically cancel out the form, it loses its meaning; only the variation of matter emerges, and with it the phenomenon of music.

So, every sound phenomenon (like the words of a language) can be taken for its relative meaning or for its own substance. As long as meaning predominates, and is the main focus, we have literature and not music. But how can we forget meaning and isolate the in-itself-ness of the sound phenomenon?

There are two preliminary steps:

Distinguishing an element (hearing it in itself, for its texture, matter, color).

Repeating it. Repeat the same sound fragment twice: there is no longer event, but music.

May 15. The problem of the train is very different from that of the bells. The manipulation of the bells removed from them their identity as bells. They became unidentifiable. I had obtained a musical element that was pure, composable, and had an original timbre. With the trains I was a long way from the field of music and, in effect, trapped in the field of drama. Now, if I take an "extract" from the train and demonstrate its existence by repetition, I get a material that can be composed, which calls for a certain type of music. So suddenly both problems find a common solution, except that the "bell" element presents as a fairly pure sound, whereas the "train" element is a "sound complex" with a poorly defined rhythmic and melodic makeup.

For the "concrete" musician there is no difference between the cut bell and the piece of train: they are "sound fragments." For the classical musician there is a difference due to habit. He could, just about, compose a score for a cut bell, which could theoretically be played note by note on the gramophone. To compose a "Railway Study," on the other hand, you have to isolate the various sound fragments, manipulate them, and link these "sound complexes" together. Algebra of the note, geometry of the fragment, is what these two musics are, if indeed there are two.

Similarly, architecture is not bothered about chemically pure materials but about their form. If I put stones together, I will be interested not so much in their striations and veins as in their volumes and alignments. So the internal rhythm of a "train" element that, from the music theory point of view, is very important becomes negligible when this element forms the elementary material of a composition.

I have coined the term *Musique Concrète* for this commitment to compose with materials taken from "given" experimental sound in order to emphasize our dependence, no longer on preconceived sound abstractions, but on sound fragments that exist in reality and that are considered as discrete and complete sound objects, even if and above all when they do not fit in with the elementary definitions of music theory.

May 25. One month spent on this "Etude aux chemins de fer" (Railway study). The result is monstrous the more the two methods are juxtaposed. Because of their "popular appeal" I haven't dared to abandon the dramatic sequences, but secretly I hope that one day there will come together an audience that prefers the theoretically less rewarding sequences, where the train must be forgotten and only sequences of sound color, changes of time, and the secret life of percussion instruments are heard.

May 26. I have obtained some quite remarkable transformations by playing a fragment recorded at 78 rpm at 33 rpm. By playing the record at rather less than half speed, everything goes down a bit more than an octave and the tempo slows at the same rate. With this apparently quantitative change there is also a qualitative phenomenon. The "railway" element at half speed isn't the slightest bit like a railway. It turns into a foundry and a blast furnace. I say foundry to make myself understood and because a little bit of "meaning" is still attached to the fragment. But very soon I perceive it as an original rhythmic group, and I am in constant admiration at its depth, its richness of detail, its somber color.

I conclude from this that concrete music will differ from classical music on another important point. In classical music a *do* is a *do* whatever its situation in the tessitura. In concrete music a sound, generally "complex," cannot be separated from its situation in the sound spectrum. It is part of its quality; nothing can be superimposed, divided, transposed.

May 28. Although I'm working hard, I've given up my original plan, any idea of a "Symphony." "Study" is a more appropriate title for my attempts at composition, each one concentrating on a particular area. The studio is no longer full of an unusable miscellany of objects. It's all happening in the sound booth. For example, I only need to record an empty tin can rolling about for a bit. I can work from this recording for hours, and the sound is so transposed and unrecognizable that the tin can disappears. Indeed, from a box of matches can come melody, harmony, percussion . . . Sound material in itself has inexhaustible potential. This power makes you think of the atom and the reservoir of energy hidden in its particles, ready to burst out as soon as it is split. Instead of composing a series of studies I would do well, if I were logical and worked without bothering about an immediate result, to record only "samples," each one taken from an initial noise. After all, isn't this noise the same as an orchestra makes? In the Erard Hall I find an amateur orchestra conducted by Pierre Billard. After the clarinet, a general "A" is unleashed, adorned with embellishments that I record with care.

May 29. My experiment succeeds beyond expectation. From this multiform "A" I have drawn out interesting sound cells. This time it's really music. But it's difficult to link the various elements. And the elements call for a response. Hence the idea of a dialogue, and the use of a solo instrument that has all the instrumental resources of ordinary music.

May 30. Jean-Jacques Grunenwald has agreed to play the concertante piano. He responds with great virtuosity to the "concrete" themes with a music that I would call abstract were it not so spontaneous. It is abstract insofar as it comes from his imagination, and it is expressed through his expert fingers and obedient keyboard. Obedience is certainly not a quality of our gramophones, which send strange sequences to Grunenwald in the studio. There is, alas, a lot of background noise with these sounds, for it has to be admitted that all these manipulations ultimately do an enormous amount of damage to the sound quality, despite all the efforts of my colleague Jacques Poullin, a sound engineer.

J.-J. Grunenwald, who is in quite a hurry, leaves as soon as he has recorded his responses. I envy him for making such pleasing music in such a short time, whereas we will need a fortnight to produce links and transitions, many of which are clumsy. And so I obtain a strange tutti that is occasionally incoherent yet full of sound treasures, most of them unheard in the etymological meaning of the word.

This study for piano and orchestra is still a compromise. The dialogue between the concrete elements and J.-J. Grunenwald's piano is shaky: two such different worlds cannot work together so easily. In any case the experiment was worth it.

June 2. Where does the clumsiness of the *Diapason concertino* come from? Certainly not from the material itself, since J.-J. Grunenwald's concertante piano responds to sequences that themselves were taken from orchestral matter. So it must be that concrete manipulations *create forms* that clash with the usual musical style.

I have a new proof of this with the *Etude aux tourniquets.* At the time of the very first experiments, faced with the impoverishment of bits of wood, I turned to Gaston Litaize and asked him to develop the themes for two whirligigs and three zanzis livened up with a xylophone and a ring of bells, relying on the score to bring it out of its impoverishment. Although I had given him a complete outline in theory (fig. 1), I had great difficulty in obtaining a short score from Gaston Litaize, out of friendship rather than real enthusiasm. Indeed, the results were pathetic, despite the goodwill of the zanzi and whirligig players, all Conservatoire prizewinners. The bar lines, which Gaston Litaize had imposed somewhat aggressively on the whirligigs and zanzis, destroyed all their charm. In vain I had suggested that the handles of the whirligig should be turned irregularly

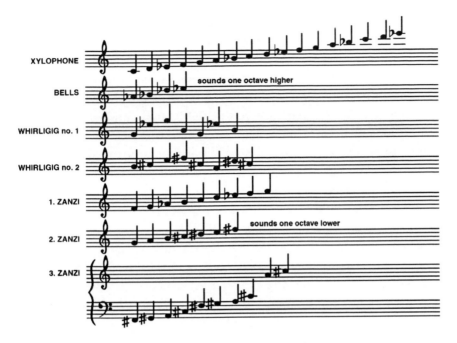

FIGURE 1. [Tablature of the *Etude aux tourniquets.*]

and the zanzi blades be used for their indeterminate tonality. Gaston Litaize wanted to impose order on everything, and the objects had resisted. The performance itself smacked of the baton, the ruler of strictly measured playing. Gazelles die like this, behind bars.

When, some weeks later, I again took up the record that witnessed to these pointless efforts, I had the idea of treating it as raw material from which I could take extracts. Ignoring the score, I took short pieces, preferably from all the "odd moments" of the performance. I chose the most interesting. Then the whole process of concrete music took place: transformation of these fragments by varying speed, timbre etc. . . . Then synthesis. Thus was born the real *Etude aux tourniquets,* a radioactive isotope of the previous one, this time neither impoverished nor childish but amazing and densely packed. The musical ideas from the original score disappeared almost entirely, because the splices created new structures that had no connection with the original compositional intention. If some initial elements were recognizable, they were like fossils, where ultimately only their chemical composition interests us. So the proliferation of forms cancels out form, which turns back into matter.

June 4. There is no instrument on which to play concrete music. That is the main difficulty. Or else we have to imagine a huge cybernetic-like machine that can achieve millions of combinations, and we're not there yet. As long as I have no more than two or four turntables that make only approximate transitions, I shall remain horribly imprisoned in a discontinuous style where everything seems to have been hacked out with a billhook. Is there a compromise?

I instinctively turn to the piano. The preceding manipulations have in fact taught me that a piano could well replace all sound effects equipment. You can strike the strings directly, or scratch or lightly stroke them, but you can also use the keyboard, not as a musical instrument, but as a convenient way of attacking the strings, which will have undergone some "preparation."[1] So every note on the keyboard has a more or less musical sound or noise, which can be quite precisely regulated. In this instance the keyboard is no longer a modulating instrument but must be considered a commutating instrument.

However, playing the "prepared piano" does not, for all that, lead to concrete music; the characteristics of instrumental play remain and preserve traditional forms: play is always more or less in time and melodic. Nevertheless, acoustically amplified, the piano can become a super–percussion section. So, using the piano as both a percussion instrument and a source of concrete sound leads to a technique that, of course, does not resolve the previous difficulties but to a certain extent turns them around.

If I ask Pierre Boulez to record a series of chords in different styles (classical, romantic, impressionist, atonal, etc. . . .) on a given theme, I can, by manipulating this "sound stuff," construct groups that will still have something in common with the initial sound but without being

---

1. The term "prepared piano" was used systematically by the American John Cage, whose works I was unaware of at this time. The use of the piano is similar in both cases, but with John Cage it leads to a music that still remains fairly abstract in its conception and performance.

recognizable as clearly as the whirligigs. At least these series will have the merit of providing an element of continuity, even a melodic development, whereas the concrete, concertante fragments will still have their discontinuous character. The merit of these initial piano studies is that we avoided having to use the "prepared piano," which later was to create effects that were more brilliant but less pure. And so the *Etude violette* and its twin sister the *Etude noire* came into being, the first more uneven, the second more melodic.

June 6. Now that the decks are cleared, real work can begin. There have been so many materials over the last four months that simply using them could take as long again. More than five hundred records are unworked stone, ore that must be refined. And precisely at this moment I am being sent on a mission to Washington. I must abandon the fruits of this long labor, which I have scarcely glimpsed. And the works that I have sketched out seem hardly usable, for any audience!

This worries me constantly. What will the radio administrators think of this mess of records, this apparent waste of time, this "Symphony" not even begun?

On this evening of my departure I can't resist coming in for a final studio session. I am making a last attempt to be clear in my mind about *voices*.

The inclusion of vocal elements has tempted me for a long time. I have no actors and even fewer singers (but for weeks I've been doing without performers). There are still old forgotten records lying around in a studio. The one that comes to hand contains the wonderful voice of Sacha Guitry. "On your lips, on your lips . . . ," says Sacha Guitry. But the recording has been interrupted by the continuity girl's coughing, which explains why the record was rejected. I grab this record, I put the deeply peaceful rhythm of a good old barge on another turntable, and then whatever comes to hand on two other turntables: an American accordion or mouth organ record and a Balinese record. Then follows an exercise in virtuosity with the four potentiometers and the eight switches.

Fortune favors fools: *Etude no. 5,* called *with saucepans* (because this study begins and ends with a sequence from a spinning tin can), is done in a few minutes, the time needed to record it.

In the four preceding studies you can see how much the development leaves to be desired, how clumsy the crescendos are and how unskilled the transitions. In the *Etude aux casseroles* (Saucepan study) the French canal barge, the American mouth organ, the priests from Bali miraculously begin to obey the god of turntables; they form a skilled group, in charge of its effects; and when the insistent "On your lips" (three times) interrupted by coughing occurs, the listener, invited to listen for the first time, is rightly astonished by a composition so skilled, so harmonious, so masterly. This is how the classics of concrete music come about.

3

*On international conferences as a concrete concert. Absent
friends are not always wrong. Nature never repeats itself.
The article from* Polyphonie. *Is there an abstract concrete cycle?*

Hurriedly abandoning the studio for the plane, I was not to have anything more to do with concrete music for a year. I was going from a con-
fined atmosphere to broader horizons, and from a problem so specific
that it seemed to concern me alone to problems so general that they required the presence of delegates from all over the world. These delegates
from Atlantic City, Copenhagen, Mexico were going to share wavelengths
among the ninety countries on the planet. Months, years were going by
without the slightest chance of agreement. In short, I was going from a
difficult technique to an insoluble policy. Sometimes, in the course of
endless sessions, I would listen to the delegates' pronouncements with a
"concrete ear" and perceive all the better their perfectly illogical workings. No argument could convince anybody, and other laws governed
persuasion: the patience of some, the violence of others, the endurance of
one group, the cleverness of another; it was all about who could get the

last quarter of an hour. Four booths of interpreters labored away completely pointlessly translating the speeches. You could hear the Russian without understanding him: an insistent melody and a multiple and inexhaustible rhythm are more convincing than the meaning of the words. The Anglo-Saxons operated in blocks of blunt syllables, suave or sharp halftones. The South Americans spoke with their hands, conducted orchestras, so comfortable with artifice, so expressive, that any more and we would have thought them sincere. And among other, indigenous, musics, those that we foolishly accuse of exoticism, African, Hindu, Arab—truthfully, almost the only disciples of Descartes—defended fair shares, the geometrical mean—in short, a so-called "Western" rationalism. They alone in this concert were worthy of the Médaille de solfège (Medal for musicianship) and the Prix de Rome.

In common with concrete music these international conferences were resolutely empirical. They too made a great noise in which, as in the case of the railway, variety had to be sought out amid endless monotony.

What happened during this year of inactivity? On Tuesday, October 5, 1948, the first "Noise Concert" had been broadcast, not on an experimental station, but on the station that was theoretically most popular: the "Parisian." I expected complaints; I rather dreaded scandal. Twelve letters arrived, friendly and enlightened.

> . . . I was overcome by the symbols, the richness, the diversity, and the novelty of some of the groupings . . . —Y. L.

> . . . I must tell you straightaway about the profound, deep-seated emotion I felt while listening, and which I still feel, as in those compelling dreams that are only dispelled long after we awake and that we never entirely forget . . . It was as if I were listening to superb Balinese music; the music that you could imagine coming from the center of an atom: the ultrasonic music created maybe by the movement of the planets: the music that Poe and Lautréamont and Raymond Roussel would hear inwardly. The noise concert is not only the first concert of surrealist music;[1] it contains, in my opinion, a musical revolution . . . —G. M.

---

1. In fact, the Italians, with Marinetti, were precursors twenty years before this. But they were concerts of direct noises, leading, as we have seen, to a dead end.

... An amazing explosion in which the dream finds its proper place ...
A new way which will deliver us from the stagnation and deadlock into
which slowly, surely, poetry is sinking ... —C. C.

Two of these letters already contained in embryonic form an indication
of the two different paths that concrete music could have followed. One
is from a film director, the other from a music composer:

> ... These sound treasures must next be organized with a goal in view,
> focused and classified; as far as possible the *other norm* of sound art, as
> opposed to musical art, must be sought ... —M. P.

> ... Should a noise work have form or not? I think so; your *"étude pathé-
> tique"* left me with the most vivid memory because of its form (perhaps,
> as well, because of the greater use of "pure" noises). I think that one
> could start by using existing musical forms, of course reserving the right
> to create new forms adapted to this new music ... —M. C.

The problem was clearly stated: is there a case for seeking out a new
sound domain on the borders of music, or, on the contrary, should these
new concrete music materials, presuming they finally become more
malleable, be incorporated into a musical form?

My correspondents also explained their projects to me.

> ... A radio work: *Bruits et voix de mon corps* (Sounds and voices of my
> body)—particularly the unheard, inaudible, internal sounds ... *Ce que le
> ciel écoute* (What the sky listens to)—from the hertzian wave to the wind,
> the sounds of the earth ... —M. P.

> ... I remember having done an experiment *in music* that could perhaps
> be relevant to you. As conductor for Radio Bucharest, I used one of my
> rehearsals to do the following: we detuned all the stringed instruments.
> For example, the violinist on the right of the desk was tuned F, E, G♯, D;
> his colleague on the left of the desk G♭, D, G, E♭ ... I transposed all the
> wind instruments: horns in A were in F, trumpets in D played in C. Then
> we played the first part of Beethoven's Seventh Symphony. The result
> was astonishing: we created an almost new work (there was nevertheless
> a bit of Beethoven here and there), and this new work had a value of its
> own because of the form of the symphony ... —M. C.

The study called *"pathétique"* had the acclaim of all my critics. They
acknowledged the technical qualities of the study called "with piano."

But a sort of unanimity had spontaneously arisen to exclude the study called "concertante." Finally, the best-informed correspondents appreciated in the *Etude aux chemins de fer* and the *Etude aux tourniquets,* the effort to abstract the noise from its dramatic context and raise it to the status of musical material.

Most of the letters asked for clarification. I decided to give them a journal, the day-by-day account of my various activities, as it was too soon to formulate any theory. This journal appeared in a special edition of *Polyphonie* on "mechanized music."

It gave an account, as I have just done, of the beginnings of concrete music, together with some diagrams that it might be useful to reproduce here.

One is in effect the first attempt to make a concrete music score. It represents the most interesting sequence of the *Etude aux chemins de fer* but also perfectly illustrates the concept of fragment or musical object and its substitution for the concept of note or pure sound. The sequence in question was composed of several "series of fragments" such as the series I, 1/I, II, 1/II, etc. . . . (fig. 2 [pp. 26–27]).

The part of the composition used here can be summed up thus. Take, for example, fragments *a, b, c, d,* chosen for their decreasing durations, each of which can, by and large, suggest a 4/4, 3/4, and 2/4 bar, respectively, and in one tempo, then "punctual" elements *e, f, g.* A series *a, b, c, d, e, f, g* would probably have no expressive character at all. After all, nature can provide a series like this without any discernible creative involvement. (Perhaps when I talk about fragments, you are wondering which fragments I mean. It doesn't matter, but, to focus the mind, let us say they're taken from coach rhythms, but it's of no consequence; it can be any sound at all.)

If I compose a series doubling each fragment *aa, bb, cc, dd,* then quite clearly there appears a will that can under no circumstances be mistaken for a chance encounter. *Nature never repeats the same thing twice.* I can then follow this series of double fragments with the simple series *e, f, g,* because the series without repetition will take its willed character from what comes before.

If I then compose another series with the same structure out of elements that I notate with the number 2, I obtain a variation on "theme" I.

Again, it could be something quite different from the elements obtained from the train rhythms. It is clear that, whatever the sound material arising from pure chance, a will to compose is manifest in the imposition of structure. To put it another way, the same thing has been repeated twice.

This should also be noted: as soon as a draft structure has been notated, a host of combinations may take shape; and it would be easy to yield to the temptation of paper, which is contrary to the spirit and the method, and even the potential, of concrete music. However constructed these sequences may appear, a listener, in the act of hearing, will sense a vague organization but will be nowhere near to perceiving its rigor. The pursuit of such a Cartesian rigor in construction, as well as coming up against insoluble instrumental problems, is no guarantee of aesthetic effect. It would be strange if concrete music could be constructed from a geometrical diagram. The ear—and the inspiration it conducts—is sensitive to combinations of figures that are more complex and more "irrational," in a different sense, than the figures on my little drawing.

The article in *Polyphonie* contained another diagram that showed the two musics in parallel and with their symmetrical stages:

ORDINARY MUSIC	NEW MUSIC
(so-called abstract)	*(so-called concrete)*
PHASE I. Conception (mental)	PHASE III. Composition (material)
PHASE II. Expression (notated)	PHASE II. Drafts (experimentation)
PHASE III. Performance (instrumental)	PHASE I. Materials (making)
(from the abstract to the concrete)	*(from the concrete to the abstract)*

The adjective "abstract" is applied to ordinary music because it is initially conceived in the mind, then notated theoretically, and finally executed in an instrumental performance. As for "concrete" music, it is made up of preexisting elements, taken from any sound material, noise, or musical sound, then composed experimentally by direct montage, the result of a series of approximations, which finally gives form to the will to compose contained in rough drafts, without the help of an ordinary musical notation, which becomes impossible.

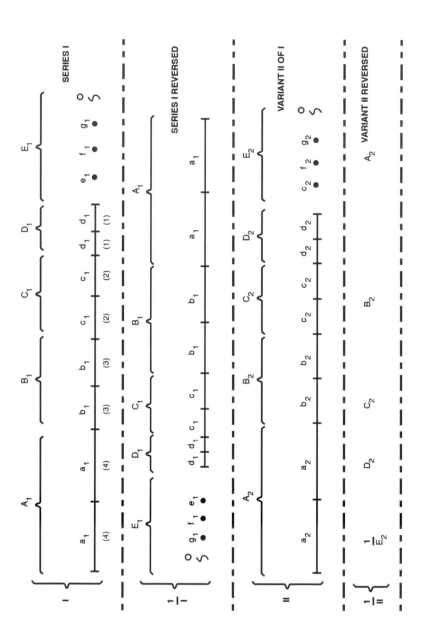

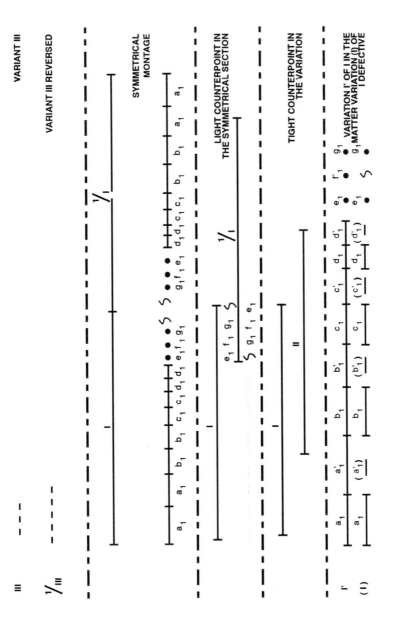

FIGURE 2. [Serial structures of the *Etude aux chemins de fer*.]

These two diagrams [on p. 25 and pp. 26–27] can be studied first of all for their fundamental differences. They can also be studied for their relationship to each other, that is, it is possible to see prefigured the process of exchange that could one day take place between the ancients and the moderns. It would no longer be a matter of seeing two movements, equal but opposed, but of seeing a cycle that could be set down thus:

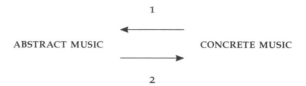

Arrow number 1 denotes the potential effect of experiments in concrete music on the imagination of a musician who is happy to use the traditional orchestra. It could even be said that, if his imagination fails, the musician would use the discoveries of concrete music to kick-start his inspiration. Arrow number 2 represents the preliminary contributions made by classical methods to the composer of concrete music. Ultimately, the use of the two domains simultaneously and the normal functioning of the cycle may dispose other kinds of composers to alternate the preconceived and the experimental systematically and *repeatedly*.

For myself, I could quite well see how to use arrow number 1. I could have been a composer who wanted to write an original work based on the *Etude noire* or *pathétique*, the concrete study providing both a sound model and a climate of inspiration. I could not see quite so well how to put the resources of abstract music into the service of concrete music, yet I had to do this. Interesting results had been obtained from crude noises, so better ones could be hoped for by applying the same methods to a more elevated sound matter. Should a score be composed beforehand for this? Could any existing work be used to extract fragments that it was known would become unrecognizable?

Arrow number 2, during my enforced inactivity, represented the line of force of my curiosity. It showed me the way down which I was soon to rush more or less headlong as soon as I could return to France and get a studio. Arrow number 2 led to *Suite 14*.

4

A tough summer. Economy and discretion. The Suite pour 14 instruments *(Suite for 14 Instruments). A* Prelude *that goes well. A* Courante *that is an instant success. A back-to-front* Rigodon *(Rigadoon). A disobedient* Gavotte. *The* Sphoradie. *Frozen words.*

Arrow number 2 involved a starting point, a journey, a destination. The starting point was a return to customary orchestral methods; the journey, the transformation of these by concrete procedures; the destination, a new music. The experiment in carving musical fragments from train noises, whirligigs, rolling tin cans showed that a structure was possible. It would be all the more so if I allowed myself less difficult materials to start from. At least that was my thinking when, on my return to Paris, I took over the studio again. It was August 1949, and by special dispensation, everyone being on holiday, it opened its doors to me alone.

For economy's sake, I limited my orchestra to fourteen instruments. For discretion's sake, I didn't ask anyone to write down the score. Once this score was destined for vivisection, I didn't want to cast a slur on someone else's work. I preferred to write it down in my own amateur way (it's a bit clumsy, said Jean-Michel Damase politely, as with dazzling virtuosity he helped me with the orchestration). At least I was sure of having certain effects at my disposal in advance: combinations of timbres, symmetrical arrangements that the procedures of concrete music would later take up and prolong. In this way I imagined five pieces forming a suite called *Suite 14*, the "14" referring to the basic starting point, the sounds of fourteen instruments. In fact, the composition was to be more and more disrupted, with each of the five pieces moving further away from the original score.

Apart from the intention to increasingly disrupt the original score, the idea was to use each piece for the application of a particular procedure. The first movement, entitled *Prologue*, was to remain faithful to the original composition and have only acoustic adjustments: reverberation almost to the point of echo, artificial doubling almost running into rhythmical counterpoint. The second piece, *Courante*, was a monody, distributed amongst the fourteen instruments, at first phrase by phrase, then cell by cell, and even note by note. It was difficult to perform, especially at a rapid pace. I was relying on acceleration to give virtuosity to the whole thing. A number of cells, cut out from this monody, would then be assembled vertically or horizontally. The third movement was a *Rigodon*, very rhythmical, at a cheeky pace, with drums and trumpets to accentuate the rhythms. I specifically wanted to disarticulate this *Rigodon* to bring in sound symmetries played backward, and to develop cadences announced by some trumpet sound that could be repeated, imitated, distorted in every possible way. As for the *Gavotte*, the fourth piece in the *Suite*, the initial score consisted of a very consonant short phrase with a dozen variations, each variation played by three of the fourteen instruments. These successive trios combined timbres more and more oddly. The oddness would be reinforced by a certain number of complete transpositions, for example, by multiplying or dividing the playback speed, affecting both tessitura and tempo, in a relationship determined in advance.

In short, it was a series of studies rather than a suite. In the first four movements quite a lot of emphasis was placed on experimenting with procedures; the fifth and last movement was the real essay in expression. To emphasize that the author had complete freedom, it was called *Sphoradie.*

It was a miserable holiday. Sometimes, as if to pull myself together during that radiant month of August, I played the five sides of the records on which the initial score was recorded. A waste of time . . .

All around me lay piles of records bearing fragments of this raw material, decomposed, compressed, and stretched, de-ossified, inverted, shattered, pulverized. I was like a child who has taken the growl out of his teddy bear, pulled out his dolly's eyes, and smashed his clockwork train. I had to admit that I had invented amazing techniques for destruction but that every attempt at synthesis fell to bits in my hands. Furthermore, at every stage of my activities, pitiless contradictions arose. Sound objects multiplied, but their proliferation brought no enrichment, at least not in the way that musicians mean: the musical idea, or shadow of an idea that persisted throughout these contortions, remained unchanged, and what a lot of misshapen forms, and *concrete* variations for the same idea! The variations themselves were contradictory, too musical and not musical enough—too musical because the banality of the original composition persisted, not musical enough because most of these sound objects were harsh, offensive to the ear.

Would I have to give up? Even if, two years later, it becomes clear that the cause of some of these contradictions is perfectly comprehensible, how can one be clairvoyant when in mid-experiment?

The paradox was that for two years I had been practising concrete music but without having yet discovered it. I had discovered operational procedures, I was capable of manipulating, and I was nowhere near being as advanced on the theoretical level. I was a prisoner of my closed grooves. A famous song by Edith Piaf illustrates the closed groove. Before becoming a method it appeared as a "gimmick," a sound "effect." But from being an effect, it can become a cause and a means of discovery. The latter arises from a symbolic difference: the difference between a spiral and a circle. It turns out that the disc cutter is a machine that draws its own symbol (fig. 3). The cutter's spiral is not only the material realization but also the affirmation of time going by, time gone by, which will never come again. If the cutter closes its magic circle in on itself, one

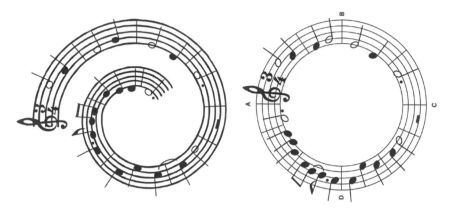

FIGURE 3. [Recording spiral (symbolic representation).]

FIGURE 4. [Closed groove (symbolic representation).]

of two things can happen: either it is an accident, and, when the inattentive operator notices it, he finds the machine damaged because the cutter has scratched the record right to the heart (for every record has a metallic "heart" that is easily harmed when the thin layer of lacquer is pierced); or he has done it deliberately, and, skilfully raising the cutter once the groove has "bitten its tail," he has isolated a "sound fragment" that has neither beginning nor end, a sliver of sound isolated from any temporal context, a clean-edged time crystal, made of time that now belongs to no time (fig. 4)—when played, the closed groove can start at A, B, C, or D. But where it began is soon forgotten and the sound object appears in its entirety, with neither beginning nor end.

When, by an extraordinary stroke of inventive genius, Rabelais imagines "frozen words" in *Pantagruel*, he does more than foreshadow the recording of sound. Swearing, shouting, the neighing of horses, the clash of arms, yells, screams of terror are suddenly isolated and set hard, separated from History, and piled up, frozen, in a chaos of oblivion. The warmth of a hand melts them and they are tossed around like stones. Here time past is not just reconstituted; it bursts out. Depending on Pantagruel's mood, the thousand bits of sound compose a different symphony, not in the order in which they occurred, but as the hand picks them up, or in any order imposed upon them.

I had been right to use the *Courante* for an in-depth trial of the closed groove. The fact that I had a monody and not a polyphony simplified the experiment and allowed me to observe more clearly. We had become used to making these grooves, and Jacques Poullin and I set about it with a will. So, like spontaneous generation in full fermentation, we spawned a number of little "motifs," the issue of the original monody, and among them there were some very remarkable ones. A statistician could have enjoyed himself counting how many of these children of chance had received some precious gift: rhythm, intonation, expression, surprise. Statistics could have recorded the percentage of grooves having particular rhythmic or melodic characteristics, the percentage with rational note values, or even the percentage of grooves that could not be notated in quavers or semiquavers. Another peculiarity of these little sound creatures was that in some way they eluded the language of music. Initially assembled to make phrases, they had escaped like the words from a dictionary and were going tirelessly round and round on the turntables all by themselves. This phenomenon could well appear unimportant to the inattentive ears of so many professional musicians. Poets, much more aware, opened theirs up. A similar thing had already happened to words. Freed from the label "realistic" and taken for themselves in their chance or artificial encounters, words had provided enough experimental material over some decades to make people take notice. So, while musicians started to grumble, poets displayed a well-informed curiosity. It didn't matter that these sound objects resisted all syntax, expressed nothing. They came hot off the press, landing on the ear with no conceptual baggage. If they showed little grace in letting themselves be manipulated, it was perhaps that we were ungracious in forcing them. Perhaps these sound objects were meant never to return to this courante—even a concrete one—that was made from them? Perhaps their vocation as objects was to appear in some herbarium, one of those catalogues provided for the amateur, and that he consults, only too pleased that these objects are offered in a logical order and not according to some perfectly pointless and subjective author's whim?

Can we say that one mushroom is better grown than another? That a lizard is superior to a tortoise? Taste determines the choice. But science alone establishes a hierarchy of the kingdoms. Because we hadn't got the science, we were at the stage of preferring one groove to another, as a lizard might be preferred to a tortoise. There were quick ones, slow ones, pallid ones, brilliant ones. There were unforgettable ones that never would have been heard while they were surrounded, stuck in their original matrix. Already drugged by this new substance, we "played" them, showed them to each other when they seemed well formed . . .

Surprisingly the new courante—made, as we have seen, out of bits and pieces—turned out to be a success and displayed a distinctly dodecaphonic tendency. Was this nothing more than chance or contamination? Or was there an explanation? To some extent, it was both. It could be said that the cutting out had completely destroyed the tonality, though very marked, of the initial score. In reality it was rather the disjointed facture of the new courante that made it resemble a piece by Webern. As it all went very quickly and the cells were much more unexpected than the original phrases, performance was like one of those performances fraught with difficulties, where the conductor is not at all sure that everyone will come together at the double bar line. Similar adventures have been seen in dodecaphonic concerts . . .

But the experiment was to become more complicated with the *Gavotte*. No closed grooves in the *Gavotte*. Only transpositions. But large- and small-scale. A rather scholarly schema had been drawn up, establishing precise relationships between these transpositions: fifths and sixths, twelfths and twenty sevenths. To my great surprise, these intervals were no longer relevant. From the moment we were sure that the variations had obediently locked on to the theme, the transposition interval and the tonality no longer mattered. Nor did the "modulation" effect: there remained a sort of permanence, as in a piece of music emerging through a geological catastrophe that has disrupted all its layers (fig. 5). In the *Courante*, the "musical word" detached itself from the phrase and existed in its own right. In the *Gavotte*, the phrase detached itself from the piece and rose to the heights, descended to the depths. The steps of the scale were no longer of importance, nor was the tempo. An accelerando reply fol-

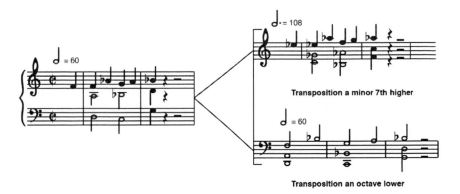

FIGURE 5. [Example of total transposition (*Suite* 14).]

lowed a rallentando without clumsiness: the piece continued. Nothing is as indestructible as a musical structure. Nothing is as independent.

As for sound played backward—we had done this experiment many times before—it bore no relationship to sound played the right way around. Not only because the structure of the sound was changed, but because the development of the musical discourse, deeply attached to the sense of time, was not reversible. With the exception of certain structures prepared in advance, such as the ones I had written for the *Rigodon,* there was no apparent connection between a fragment of sound and its reverse version, at least within the usual dimensions of customary music. On the contrary, within the dimensions of concrete music, and at that level of analysis, the forward and reverse fragments could very well form structures and contrasts, and their symmetry could be perceived.

The *Sphoradie* was at first judged unacceptable by its first listeners and defended only by the author. It must be said that everything in it shocked the ear. After an "exposition" of closed grooves cut out from full orchestral sound, in, as it were, violent snatches, you suddenly came upon a Franck-like string quartet that gradually turned back to front, then back to its true romanticism. After all, in a hundred years—if any trace of such things remains, and if ears have had the time to get used to them— who will make any distinction between sound played forward and sound played backward, which will be used as well? But it must be admitted that the first experiments are testing. After a few fade-ins and fade-outs, of which the least that can be said is that they elicited the disapproval of both camps, ancient and modern, *Sphoradie* ended with an extension of the tessitura in both directions: extremely high violins, taken from a harmonic, vertiginously bestrode a bass ostinato, whether from a piano or a kettledrum could no longer be determined. The author had made that concession to the public, and his detractors concurred in finding the end of this *Sphoradie* sublime, and he willingly handed it over to them . . .

5

Stage effects or creation? Distortion or transformation? The stumbling block of concrete music. Splitting of the musical atom. Matter and Form? Wherein the order of magnitude dictates quality. Incompetence of musicians.

In short, audiences for *Suite 14* fell into three groups. The first, after listening to the *Prelude* and *Courante*, had their minds put at rest. Claude Arrieu grumbled, "Writing isn't enough for you, you're composing! Go and play these two pieces at the Colonne concerts, they're as good as most . . . ," rather as one might say, "You used to sing? Well, now dance!" For the *Courante*, although as highly worked as split bamboo, was still bamboo. After the *Rigodon,* it all fell apart. It's all right applying concrete procedures to noise. But distorting music right to the limit presented musicians with such a caricature of their art that they were really angry, and they were not wrong. The second group of music lovers, who hadn't got much to learn from the *Prelude* and the *Courante,* acknowledged some experimental merit in the subsequent pieces but felt annoyed . . . We'd expected something from noises, but you're already turning tail, you're going back to the musical and clumsily at that! As for the third group, I think I was it: it was the group of those of two minds. In the *Sphoradie*, between those dizzying chasms that separated two worlds, I was the only one, not to feel comfortable, but for the moment to chance several perilous leaps: my fade-in–fade-outs, somewhere between Franck and gut-wrenching inversions, seemed to me to point to the future.

Of course, I realized, too late to redeem that long month of endeavor, that I had been wrong to use an orchestra, to write a score in which every note remained indelible, every phrase imperishable, every form indestructible. It was clear now that if the musical was there at the outset, it would most likely still be there at the end, and, in effect, where I most expected to find a creative phenomenon I might find only stage effects. A machine can only work on what it has: the initial material informs the whole result. From the moment I fed notes and phrases, harmonies and melodies into its jaws, it gave back the words, the phrases, more or less well digested. It was the same language, but instead of the primitivism I had expected, I got distortion and decadence.

At that time I came very near to giving up the whole enterprise.

Where, indeed, could novelty and originality come from? I only gradually fully understood this.

My first step was to reject musical material, to acknowledge that my mistake had been in going back to musical instruments, musical notation, musical thought patterns. Going back to noise would in fact have been the surest way to find solid, and at least unexplored, ground.

But if, for example, I took a creaking door, an animal cry, a thunderclap, wouldn't I find myself faced yet again with the same difficulty? I had already experienced it with the railways: I needed to tear noise away from its dramatic context and, in the same way, musical sound from the prison of notes, of the words and phrases of musical language.

In other words, even if noise material guaranteed me a certain margin of originality compared to music, in both cases I was brought back to the same problem: tearing sound material away from any context, dramatic or musical, before giving it form. If I succeeded, there would be concrete music. If not, there would be nothing but stage and radio sound effects.

Now, the closed groove had given me the feeling that I was possessed of an undeniably powerful analytical tool. Despite its discontinuous character—reminiscent of early surrealist collages—the closed groove had freed from matter as difficult as the "pure coach" elements of montage, which, unquestionably, lent themselves to being constructed without any idea of imitation. But in *Suite 14*, with the exception of the *Courante*, I was abandoning the closed groove, running away from its discontinuous character, hoping to achieve the desired continuity once I had applied the procedures to more extensive pieces.

In doing so I was turning my back, if not on concrete music, then on its future potential. I needed a new resource for invention, as important as the one that had inspired me on the day I had cut off the attack from the bells.

This time invention took place not in experimentation but in my thoughts. It had nothing to do with manipulation, but with method. A very simple and very general schema easily demonstrates this.

Imagine, then, that we start with a "form" symbolically represented by a drawing. The coordinates of this curve are very vague: they can be time in abscissa and tessitura in ordinate. So it is a melodic diagram. But what follows is so general that it really applies to any form, that is to say, every development of one element varies in relation to another. It would be as valid in space as in time, if, instead of temporal functions, as could be the case in concrete music, we had spatial functions, as in a plastic application of this theory.

So then I imagine that I conduct a series of manipulations, distortions, transfers, etc. on this "form."

I will then obtain, from an initial form F (fig. 6), forms F_1, F_2, F_3, etc., which will nevertheless be reminiscent of form F. This, generally speaking, is what happened in the *Suite 14* (second, third, and fourth movements).

If, instead of these "distortions," cuts *ab, cd, ef*, etc. are made in form F (fig. 7), and different arrangements and combinations are made with these cuts, we obtain forms S (fig. 8), which this time are perceptibly different from the initial form F. Generally speaking, the form as such is no longer recognizable. The matter, on the contrary, remains.

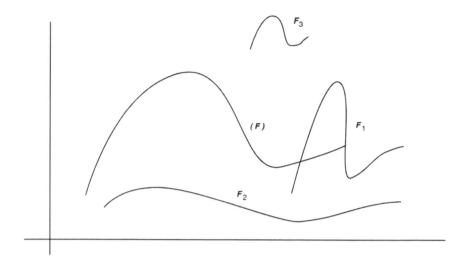

FIGURE 6. [Distortion of an initial form.]

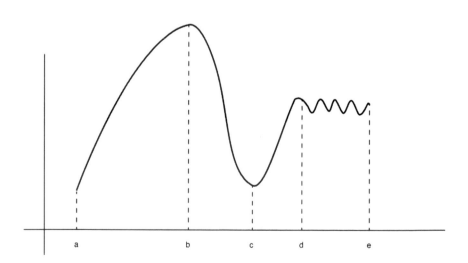

FIGURE 7. [Breakdown of a form into fragments.]

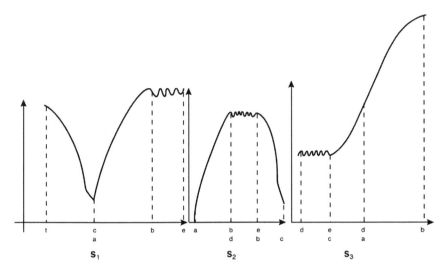

FIGURE 8. [Transformation of an initial form.]

Now let us improve on the procedure. The manipulations F1, F2, F3 were macroscopic. The process that leads to S1, S2, S3 . . . was the beginning of an analysis followed by synthesis, but on a coarse, intermediate level. If I take the analysis and synthesis on to a more refined, microscopic or infinitesimal, level, my arrangements and combinations will go beyond transformations, I will obtain transmutations. Beyond the form, I will have power over the matter itself. A closed groove belongs to this latter group. If my analysis is in the region of one-tenth of a second, this changes everything. Everything can become unrecognizable. It is at this level that the bell becomes a human voice, the voice a violin, and the violin a seabird. All that is needed is patience and, of course, mechanical resources capable of dealing with the enormous increase in the number of manipulations.

This is the stumbling block of concrete music.

The difficulty is that a short demonstration such as I have just given will easily convince a scientific mind. The prestigious power of the analytical process is the basis of all modern progress. Anyone who can distinguish between a function, its derivative, or its integral knows there is a change of form and phenomenon. It is more difficult to persuade a musician of the interest, the extreme novelty, of this sort of process applied to music. Sometimes I thought it best to mock with the mockers. *L'Etude pathétique* or *aux casseroles* elicited smiles or gravity depending on the mood or the inclination of the listener. But for a musician, especially an orthodox one, what a boon! "To the saucepan!" immediately shouts the young critic, finding my explanations inadequate . . . "Even cut up into tenths of seconds, a pan will still be a pan." Wrong . . . an atom cut into pieces is no longer the same atom. It becomes another material, gives off unexpected energy. Everything, precisely, depends on the level of analysis.

Here the comparison with atomic phenomena is in fact useful. It demonstrates to both well- and insufficiently informed minds that division involves more than a change in size and results in a change in quality. If this is done in ordinary chemistry, the end result is always the same thing. If the analysis goes deeper, into atomic structure, the end result is, in effect, a "transmutation." Scientifically, our age knows enough to prove the irrational minds of alchemists right. Without taking the analogy too far, we could ask ourselves at what stage of division sound will demonstrate these qualitative phenomena. The answer is simple. As soon as around one-tenth of a second is reached, phenomena are too short to be perceived, either as sound matter or form. All analysis, followed by synthesis, which operates at this level of division, has therefore every chance of acting on both matter and form, and in so radical a way that every original element will be unrecognizable. There will be neither noise nor musical sound, neither drama nor symphony; there will be new materials for a new way of constructing sound.

I am constantly using the terms *matter* and *form*. It might well be asked exactly what they mean. In effect, the analogy with the plastic arts is striking enough, but this is more than an analogy; this time we need a precise definition that must satisfy both a scientific and an aesthetic mind. In effect, every sound phenomenon has a certain duration. In the course of this duration there are "things that develop" and things that mediate this development. Matter and form thus seem to be opposing concepts, two entities as different as stone and the geometry that sculpts it. In the plastic arts space, the pure space of the geometry of forms is readily contrasted with matter, impure matter that has a grain, a color, a density, a hardness, and which one could go on describing endlessly. But, after all, what is this matter over and above the qualitative perceptions of our senses but more space, structural geometries, this time of the infinitely small? If, instead of our eyes we used a spectroscope or the schemata of atomic scientists, a brick, stone, plaster are yet more rhythmical spaces, arrangements of numbers, of orbits, in space. So, at least in theory, matter and form are not so different: space within space, these would be our structures of matter, except when the *order of magnitude* removes all common measure from the two spaces and gives them sensory—and therefore aesthetic—qualities, with no connection between them.

What makes the problems fairly clear in plastic materials is that the orders of magnitude are very great. There is a respectable number of zeros between the dimensions of an atom and those of a statue; something like Avogadro's number, that is, a number with twenty-three zeros, more than a billion cubed, and thus almost inconceivable. In music, on the contrary, the periodic phenomena that play the part of "matter" and that constitute the time within time that every sound form is made of are very near to durations, which we can directly perceive. You can hear a thirty-two-foot reed "beating"; musical sound is born from the moment we lose ourselves in counting the beats. So there is, in music, a curious common border between matter and form. Beat the air with a vibrating rod ten times a second and you have a rhythmic form. Double the frequency and you begin to have a sound, perceived not as a form but as matter. So instead of the abyss of Avogadro's twenty-three zeros, which, in plastic materials, separates form and matter, we have no abyss at all but contiguity, very dangerous for aesthetic disinformation.

How can we be surprised if, in music, problems of form have taken on the characteristics of a chemistry of matter and not a physics of forms? In effect, all music is mainly based on the postulate of resonances, on an architecture of frequencies, frequency being the dominant element, algebraic, almost separable from the phenomenon itself so much importance does it assume. So, abstracted, stripped of its sensory context, music has always appeared to be without those plastic characteristics that today we must restore to it.

If, on the contrary, we once again begin to distinguish, in an interval of time of about one second, the phenomena that belong to that interval from those that are about one-tenth of a second, the concept of matter and form becomes clear. Below a tenth of a second—the "atomic" dimension of sound—there is no perception of form. Sound matter can in general be perfectly well defined from the content of a tenth of a second. A variety of periodic or pseudoperiodic phenomena that have taken place during this tenth of a second have every possibility of continuing to take place during the subsequent infinitesimal intervals. They are, in a way, predictable. Take, for example, the C above the A of the turning fork (440 hertz), i.e., 1,056 periods per second. In a tenth of a second there will be 105 of these periods, which is easily enough to identify the pitch of the sound. Moreover, the timbre will also be present. The strength of the note as well. The tenth of a second, therefore, contains the "matter" of the violin note. If the violin plays hemidemisemiquavers, there may be a lot of them in one second, but the matter will not change for all that: the sound will evolve from high to low, become less loud, and the timbre may change, but, in general, with continuity, so that we will have the impression that the matter has received a form, melodic, rhythmic, or of sound color.

In short, in music, matter and form are made of the same elements— frequency, intensity, duration—but these elements have the contradictory qualities of being permanent and of varying. Insofar as they are permanent, in a short space of time they constitute a matter: insofar as they evolve, in a space of time only ten times longer they give rise to forms. Every sound phenomenon, including music, definitely can and should be analyzed in this way.

To understand the extent to which we have learned to "abstract" music, we only have to compare the graphs of real sound and its musical representation. So where are the notes and the chords in the amazing tangle of oscillations? Give an oscillogram like this to a specialist to read and he will be very embarrassed. Listen to sound as a gramophone reads it, and a child will say, "It's a third, on the piano." But no one realizes how inadequate this—doubtless rapid and brilliant—response is. The child has given two pieces of information: he has given a description of the frequency, which, after all, is also easy to find on the oscillogram. And he has *recognized* the piano. Take away the known instruments and play, not to children but to good musicians, sounds that are artificial, not identifiable through habit: what confusion, then, not only of impressions and reactions but of vocabulary! Without a system of reference for instruments, for the identification of frequencies and simple rhythms, the best musicians are incompetent. As soon as a sound phenomenon of the slightest complexity is presented to them, they have no resources to describe, analyze, or evaluate it. Hence the importance of a method that can at last give a way in to the entire sound phenomenon in all its generality. And only the concepts of matter and form can achieve this.

It goes without saying that this chapter is frankly trying to anticipate the moment of *Suite* 14. The failure of this work inclined me to look in this direction, but my ideas were still far from being clear enough, and I didn't have the mechanical means to apply my analysis rigorously enough. At least another year or two were to go by before method and machines made common cause in this respect. Meanwhile, what could I do except grope around in the dark and try to make up for the lack of means by the originality of my expedients?

The paradox is that, although concrete music was viable as a method, over the subsequent years, as far as realization was concerned, it was reduced to self-mimicry, to attempts that were on the fringes of its true method. But I needed to gain time, both for ideas to mature and for machines to be thought up, built, tried out.

6

*Many called and few chosen: Symphonie pour un homme seul
(Symphony for a lone man). Pitfalls of Rhetoric. The Symphony
in all its states. Human caring. Beginning of the score.
Prosopopée (Prosopopoeia) I and II. The concert guide.*

Subsequent research therefore still had to make do with any means it
could find. The future lay in two parallel developments: extending instrumental potential by constructing new equipment, and extending
theoretical knowledge by studying fragments and their rules of composition. But first I had to secure the present, because it was difficult to stop
an experiment like this one, even though we were expecting new technical means. The present, then, meant laboring with approximations. This
was the fate of works in progress, particularly a *Symphonie* I was prepar-
ing, with a significant title: *Symphonie pour un homme seul.* It will be seen
later that the title had nothing to do with the solitude in which Jacques
Poullin and I found ourselves in the studio. But if the title could have a
double meaning, that was fair enough. We were indeed very much alone.
Looking forward to the future meant thinking up machines, making

them, trying them out. All of the musicians whom until then we had invited to join us had practically run away from a musical undertaking bristling with difficulties and defended by the barbed wire of technique. Composers, conductors, virtuosi had passed through the studio. We had also appealed to jazz musicians, trusting in their improvisatory abilities and their unconstrained sense of sound material. But jazz, even more than the classical orchestra, makes its music with nerves and muscles. The jazz musicians declined as well. Finally there appeared a young prize-winning composer from the Conservatoire with a respectable background (he had worked in the Messiaen class), who could start straightaway. A pianist but, most of all a virtuoso percussionist, he was predisposed to violence because of his frail appearance. An instinct for power, very characteristic of his generation, inclined him to maximum disruption, minimum melody and harmony. Invited for a trial session, Pierre Henry came into the Studio as so many others had done. This, as I had assumed ephemeral, passing presence was not to leave it again. The *Symphonie pour un homme seul* began with the friendship of two isolated people.

Of course the *Symphonie* was presented as a reaction to *Suite* 14. As the orchestra had played such a mean trick on me, I decided to choose my initial elements from a field opposed to music, the field of noises. I would use no mechanical noises with sharp peaks, cyclical time, and clear timbre but instead noises devoid of any formal element. I concentrated on the organic and the living. The lone man had to find his symphony within himself, not by simply thinking up music in the abstract but by being his own instrument. A lone man possesses much more than the twelve notes of the trained voice. He shouts, he whistles, he walks, he punches, he laughs, he groans. His heart beats, his breathing accelerates, he pronounces words, calls out, and others call in reply. Nothing echoes a lone cry more than the hubbub of the crowd.

Severely limited by musical expression, weary of seeking from machines help that they were powerless to give, I turned to radiophonic expression. My correspondents had anticipated this step, and I conceived the *Symphonie* without remembering that one of my first listeners had had the same idea (I realized this when going through some old letters for this little book). The inclination that leads the mind to use such resources is therefore natural.

Without some experience of concrete music I should probably have composed the *Symphonie* as a sort of poetry or radiophonic drama. The extent of the orchestration of noises would not have been enough to bring this work into the domain of musical expression. In reality, I was very divided between the two forms, as can be seen from the notes in which I outlined my project at the time. Escaping into the domain of poetry involved turning, explicitly or implicitly, to the text. Drama, even without a text, involved suggestion.

SYMPHONIE POUR UN HOMME SEUL: Plan

Title (spoken), then (spoken), Exordium!
The man gets up and yawns, like this: *Yawn.*
So, he shows his gums and you can see that he has hardly any canines left. Otherwise his yawn would be like a wild animal's, like that: *Yawn with special effects.* But this is not so different from that. It could be that they are one and the same thing.
The man, once up, begins to walk like this: *Steps.* These are the steps of a lone man. But the steps of a crowd are made of as many steps, thus: *Many steps.*
Lastly, the man is breathing and his heart beats; he is so used to it that he doesn't hear the noise it makes: *Noise (breath and heart).* It is no different from the noise of a forge or a machine: *Amplified noise.* Wild animal, crowd and thing, that is what a man is, if you listen to his chest, and this is what no one dare reveal, or let anyone hear, because it's frightening. This exploration is in darkness. You go down with winching gear, the listening device on the end of a line, a line to explore man: the man of his own caves. It may not be beautiful, it doesn't seem true when it's magnified ten times, a hundred times, but it can be instructive (strings break: it's the highest strings of the violin that break. We had deliberately overstretched them to make this happen.) Because we want to play the game: no instruments, nothing but man. Man is an instrument that is too seldom played.
And we're not dealing with words either, blow them! A man-music. A man sings, yep, he shouts, that's better: *(shout)*; he whistles, he blows into his palms, like this: *(whoo).* He stamps, beats his chest, may even beat his head against the walls.
This is what man has a right to do, what is given to him for today, to express himself if he can.

Machines will do the rest.

Oh! yes, if he picks a blade of grass on his way he has the right to use it, like this: *(grass)*.

Let's begin! First we have to put across how lone the man is, and how much he is made to walk. *(Sequence of steps.)* (At the end, section, halt, attention, stand at ease, pause.)

(Spoken) Symphony for a lone man, second item. Exordium!

As for what is specific to man, here it is: *Sequence of laughter.* (In an undertone) minim rest.

(Spoken) Third part: Exordium! Stop sniggering, Man of little faith, stop pitting your voice against mountains, learn the solitary ways. A shell against your ear will make your blood sing to the rhythm of the sea. This is because there are two universes, similar in every way, separated only by the surface of your skin; and your vacillating senses scarcely make you aware of it. *Symphonic sequence* (finishing on the word *absolute*).

Fourth part, Exordium!

How did it all start? Nothing very nice in a man's snoring. The noise of a sleeper is also the sound of a dying man. In truth there is no difference between a snore and a death rattle; has anyone pointed this out? I have. So, let's say he was sleeping like a child. God approaches. Now God, it will be remembered, created me with his breath. It is from that particular sound that I hear God. But why is He waking me up? I was sleeping like an angel. Ouch! *(amplified cry)* Good God, you're hurting me!

I had hardly got over my surprise when already . . . But yes, the wound had been closed up as at Lourdes; nothing but a little chloroform discomfort, and something other had been born of me. *(Doubling of the voice.)*

I didn't know how alone I was, and it is not good that man should be alone, God had said (repeat an octave lower). Let us give him a companion like unto himself. Oof, like! . . . Why not different, to make a bit of a change? Still me, me again. Disappointment of love. I love you, I love myself, I love only you, you of me, me of you, oh! oh! (voices).

Erotic sequence. And then, how alone one is together (two similar voices). Pause.

Fifth part: Exordium!

And man is also made to fight.

Conflict sequence. And man is made to fight (murmur in canon form, which ends with . . . And finally dies away).

Funeral sequence (interrupted by a burst of laughter, voices played backward).

Here ends the *Symphonie pour un homme seul*, made of the noises man can make, with the help of nothing, nothing in his hands, nothing in his pockets, even as we shall be at our final ending, which we shall indeed have to play alone, with no help from any equipment, and without even a microphone. Amen.

The first draft has no commentary. It may be a good radio drama. Poetico-dramatico-musical. It simply needs a broadcaster.

SYMPHONIE POUR UN HOMME SEUL: Second plan

Amboise–Paris train, X-20-51. In the fog of a headache, ideas for the *Symphonie.*

Not to go back to yesterday's dithyrambic tone; make it into something very tightly constructed, organic, fleshy. Begin with a cry?

Proportion of the commentary. Is it possible to have a commentary and still keep the surprise effect of some words like: "absolutely"?

Limit self to such a short commentary that it announces without explaining, and that it goes straight into the poem, then into the sound matter.

E.g.: After a difficult life (laughter).

Nevertheless there is love (or: there was love),

or I fall into sleep as into an egg,

or follow the guide, I'll show you round everything. Here, the aorta, the ladder goes down into the left ventricle (noises above). I go down the internal staircase with my basket of words, I stumble, they spill out everywhere, bounce about (I can only find a few of them), they were so well arranged (shower of words coming back).

There are some words, which if you dared to say them would terrify you. The word *fear*, for example. Play with words, do you know how to do that? *Jouez?* (Play?) *Prêt?* (Ready?) The first words must go, clear off into the general fuzz; waves of echoes, and, without a moment's rest,

Tour of the brains. Memory scrolls (In fast motion).

Last words (Voice played backwards).

Semisolitude (going upstairs, voices on the other side of the door, going back down, or else, solitude alone, solitude with someone else (the couple). Light and shadow. Solitude in the crowd. Inventory. Mortal solitude. Human words (the word basket). Reckoning. The Word (juggle with words).

Finally, I see:

I.   Fugue (marches, hummed themes, staircase, sound of voices, crowd),

II. Nocturne (forest, whistling),

III. Stocktaking sales (heart, lung, memory, words: I'm serious),

IV. What is specific to man (laughter etc . . .),

V.   The Word or word-play.

Could the fugue finish with man and woman? (*Verbum caro factum est—and the Word was made flesh.*)

In III, follow the panting or asthmatic voice, or grammar mistakes or shout like a deaf person, in short the inflexions of sincerity.

Accelerate or slow down. The voice disappears into its boots. (Ask the technician about the problems of modulating a noise with the voice, pebble-filter.)

First, try things out. Avoid systematic development and aim for harmony and rhythm.

The two projects were no more than two scarcely differing attempts. When the poet gets involved in music, even if it's a three-year sentence (without reprieve), he should make himself a prisoner. I did not succumb to escaping. Clutching at the bars of my cell, I remained, and, like an ascetic, I rid my project of all poetry, all scenario. This made it very much more difficult to unite inspiration and execution. Once again, I was on the verge of giving everything up, as on the day of the whirligigs and the birdcalls. The project on paper had to be slimmed down, the words disappear, become signals, symbols, and music. So no more scenario, a sort of divergent itinerary where even the intention will no longer be discerned.

SYMPHONIE POUR UN HOMME SEUL: Definitive version

I.   March;

II.   Quartet (accordion, guitar, violin, trumpet);

III. Percussion (recomposition of I.—prepared piano responses);

IV.   Vocal (elaborated hummed and articulated elements; outline of a theme);

V.   Percussion (live, as an echo);

VI.   Perpetuum (violin and prepared piano, violin perpetually going up to the highest register, piano percussion gradually descending until a violin string breaks in the highest register);

VII. Shouts (development of IV, with counterpoint of prepared piano and trumpet);

VIII. Percussion (straight, John Cage style, short and dramatic);

IX.   "And the earth was without form and void . . ."

in a voice played backward, followed by expanding circular progressions moving toward the very violent, and interrupted by short rhythmic spasms that are swallowed up and yield at the reprise.

X.   Quartet, as at II, perhaps double.

XI.   Ostinato (backward) "I think, therefore I am," counterpoint of words taken from the dictionary of rhymes with key words: organ, heart, memory . . .

XII. Duet, man's voice seeking woman's voice, light percussion accompaniment, erotic sequence, and Tahitian record,

XIII. Drum roll,

XIV. Chorale.

These sequences, one of them boldly entitled "March," were not to be realized in that form. But they were the beginning of a solution. The first being the most difficult, I had not been wrong to tackle the first sequence in the spirit of "seeing what happens," in order to have experimentally an idea of the parameters of a sound universe that would be that of the *Symphonie*. I was forced to treat sound matter in its macroscopic state, because all I had was six simple turntables, quite inadequate for an in-depth analysis of sound in concrete music. Rather than overexploit the "closed groove" effect (which nonetheless I was to use a great deal), I was inclined to work on long fragments, tracks each lasting several seconds, which did not have sound matter in a very divided state. I was looking for certain acceptable relationships between these soundtracks. Having adopted this technique, I still had to discover the principle that would govern the way the developments were constructed, unless they were completely arbitrary. Given that the *Symphonie* was to be composed from the fourteen sequences of plan no. 3, I still had to find the angle that would interlink the different soundtracks that I was going to assemble. Had I already learned the explicit lessons from *Suite 14*? Not yet, perhaps. But instinctively I did the opposite. The *Gavotte* had failed because a single musical phrase was transformed in different ways, and the meaning of this identical phrase masked the variety of the matter. So I needed to get rid of the musical phrase, that succession of words or meanings, and replace it with a series of sound objects, with no explicit meaning or plastic value. This initial series could certainly constitute a phrase, a theme, provided it did not produce variations but varieties from it. So the *Symphonie* began with a series that I considered particularly important and that I acknowledged to be absolutely arbitrary, but it was highly probable that this initial series, once given, would influence both the development of the first piece and the makeup of those that followed.

Thus, right from the first seconds, the listener was obliged to take on board a sound universe determined by certain data: sound objects were considered for themselves without the necessity of identifying them in relation to an instrument or a meaning. Although some elements were consistently vocal, others were taken from the gestures of a walker and their sound context (footsteps, tapping noises, whistling and breath). Finally, as far as the musical accompaniment as such was concerned, he found himself in the presence of altered elements that made keyboard notes into a knock on the door, using a number of effects from the prepared piano. The so-called "Cage" element—from the name of John Cage whom I had met a few weeks earlier—was a simple beating in octaves, in an interesting rhythm, on two or three prepared piano strings, not unlike four knocks on a door. The "Cage" element was itself transformed by concrete procedures until it moved toward noises that John Cage himself would not have suspected. These noises covered almost the entire range between the noise of a door and a piano keyboard. They went from the most to the least musical. If there was an orchestra, it was stretched out between the piano, an undeniably musical element, and the footsteps of a lone man, which, although they were in semiquaver rhythms on a prepared score, remained dramatic.

Assuming that the kettledrums in the Vth Symphony had served as a model, I obtained an instrumental gradation that could be notated thus:

	interior to man:	*exterior to man:*
	Elements of breathing	Footsteps or equivalent
FROM NOISE	Fragments of voices	Knocking on the door
TO MUSICAL	Cries	Percussion
SOUND	Humming	Prepared piano
	Whistled tunes	Orchestral instruments.

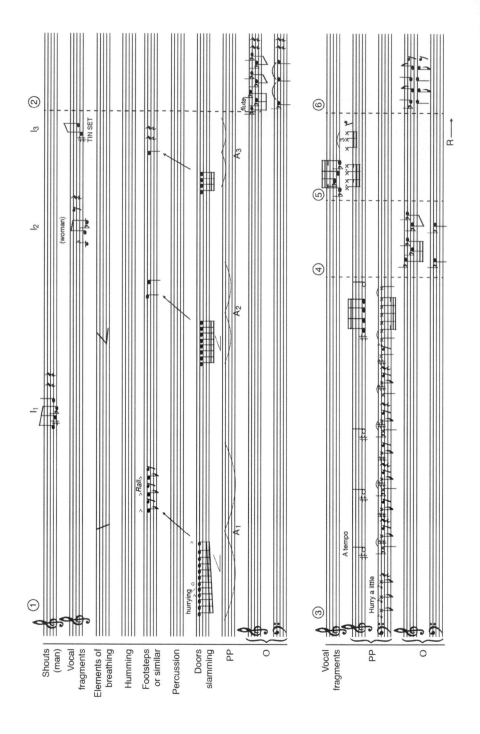

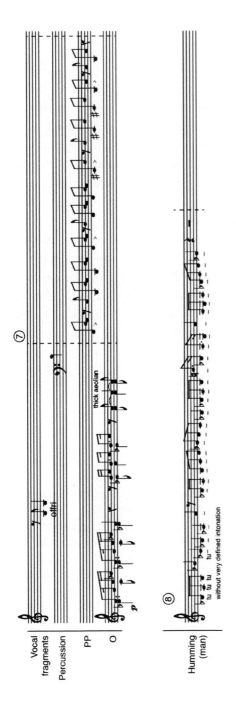

FIGURE 9. Analysis of the first sequence of *Prosopopée I (Symphonie pour un homme seul).*

1 Triple rhythmic introduction (recalling the three introductory blows of the wooden staff in the theater) A¹, A², A³, interspersed with incidental vocal fragments I¹, I², I³.

2 Orchestral fragment with a flute predominating.

3 "Cage" theme on the prepared piano.

4 Repeat of 2.

5 Variation of I (aeolian).

6 Reprise and variations of 2 ending with a loud "thick aeolian."

7 "Syncopated theme" on the prepared piano.

8 Entry of a man's voice humming.

What dominated was the marching theme, the title of the first sequence, and waiting. Then came the idea of an outside as opposed to an
inside, in physical space as much as in the psychic climate. So that listeners with dramatic inclinations could simply look for a scenario, a sort of
puzzle, while those who preferred music had time enough to enjoy a
concrete score that for the first time was fairly rigorous and where the
live elements were employed like voices accompanying an orchestra.
The balance between these elements had to be very subtle, for I only had
to cut off a few bars of footsteps, for example, for the whole sequence to
go from the dramatic to the rhythmic. So the first piece was unbaptized,
and the title *Prosopopée* replaced *March*. This is the dictionary definition
of "Prosopopée": "Rhetorical device in which inanimate objects are presented as alive." It was still a provisional title, a halfway house, as was
the work. Besides, how can a work, if it is authentic, be described in
words? This is the absurdity of all musical analysis. But custom requires
that enlightened listening should have some reading matter on the program. It was not difficult to provide something, rather like a prospectus,
for the *Symphonie* at its various performances, in concert or on the radio:

> The *Symphonie pour un homme seul* comprises, rather than the four or five
> traditional movements, about ten pieces—or "sequences"—that are con-
> nected to each other in a clearly perceptible manner, like the links of a
> chain, symmetrical or asymmetrical, contrasting or blending, depending
> on their matter or form.
>
> The first four are respectively: *Prosopopée I, Partita, Valse, Prosopopée II.*
> *Prosopopée I* establishes the setting for the whole work.
>
> *Prosopopée II,* and, between the two prosopopoeias, a transitional *Partita,*
> then a waltz, open the gates upon a universe swarming with human life,
> with the waltz of voices, deliberately scrambled, for the rhythm of voices,
> their pure presence, is enough for their music. These are followed by:
>
> *Collectif* (Collective), *Erotica, Scherzo, Cadence.*
>
> The domain of voices glimpsed in the *Valse* develops: Murmuring,
> mysterious voices in the *Collectif.* The suggestion of a single burst of laugh-
> ter in *Erotica,* and, in the *Scherzo,* the commotion of high-pitched voices.
>
> Finally, after the *Scherzo,* where the prepared piano responds to voices
> that seem to come from playtime at a village school, the *Cadence* repeats
> the most important rhythmic theme in the work.
>
> The Symphony ends with: *Eroïca, Apostrophe* (Utterance), *Strette* (Stretto).

Contrasting with the previous sequence, *Erotica, Eroïca* again has as its central motif a human noise, this time whispering as opposed to laughter, man as opposed to woman.

The *Apostrophe* seems to want to introduce an element of intelligibility into this now more tragic atmosphere.

The voices, until now scrambled, desire to escape from indistinctness and pronounce a word at last. An important word, which had initially been emphasized like a dominant in the first version of the work. But now, in the definitive version, a word henceforth pronounced rapidly and in an undertone, for anything explicit seems to be forbidden in a work of this type.

Finally, the *Strette* owes its name to the fact that it begins with a short reprise of the main elements heard previously. It develops rapidly and makes room for completely new elements that eventually attract the attention, which until then had been unfocused. These elements, mostly cyclical, intermingle, and in a series of approximations finally achieve pure stridency, crowning the whole work with its final chord.

So, the need for explanation placed the accent on the dramatic elements of the *Symphonie*. If concrete music had been part of a musical tradition, people could have written, still in the same style: "The exposition of the theme in the string section is repeated by the tutti of woodwinds. Then the first theme ends rapidly while a second theme is reprised by the horns. A rapid sforzando then interrupts the development."

The words *theme, development,* apart from suggesting a disarming facility of tempo, give this musical literature advantages that concrete music is very far from possessing.

Of course, in the *Symphonie* there was no question of exposition of theme in strings and reprise by woodwinds because there were no strings and above all no theme. It was already glorious to have Pierre Henry's prepared piano respond to vocal patterns bursting out of this mass where, for the first time, there were formal relationships. The twittering of voices interpreted in the program as the evocation of a school playground was only incidentally that school playground. They were fragments in a certain rhythm, evolving within certain limits of the tessitura, not at all like pure sounds, but like more or less bulky bursts of sound. The piano, which itself varied between normal sound and weird percussions, could be imposed on the voices in harmony or counter-point. So, from time to time, the *Symphonie* returned to the rules of music. As for the—only glimpsed—laws of concrete music, they were sometimes applied: the objects of the initial series were perfectly recognizable in their astonishing variety, and widely differing groupings of them with identifiable relationships could be found. So, for example, the *Cadence* isolated the "Cage" element and made it into an autodevelopment without needing any aid. *Prosopopée II* took up the themes of *Prosopopée I,* with variations. The *Scherzo* and the *Collectif* used voices in two different ways, one in the upper register, the other in the lower. Certainly, some motifs were recapitulated, forming bridges between *Strette* and *Eroïca.* Some pieces, such as *Erotica* and *Valse,* constituted independent parentheses and abruptly introduced a little element of originality, for a moment imposing their individual domains. The overall climate, restated in *Apostrophe,* was revealed in one word, one only, as naked as the man himself, a word spelled out slowly, laboriously. . . . And perhaps no word was needed at all, not even this perfectly enclosed word: *absolument.* This choice had probably been determined by the memory of a conversation I had with Claudel: "French has no inbuilt stress." Claudel sniggered: "No stress? It has as much as you want. You can say Ábsolument, or absólument or even abso-lumÈnt . . ." This word, for ten years, went through and through my mind, claiming its three stresses and their triple degree of freedom. Doubtless this was one of youth's last errors, an influence from which the *Symphonie* would finally set me free. As for the *Strette,* it was an apotheosis of noises in the highest register, extraordinary noises, worthy of Rimbaud and the "Sonnet des Voyelles" (Sonnet on Vowels). Pierre Henry, who went valiantly from the studio to the recording booth, was making his debut in concrete music with a burst of sound so remarkable that I immediately chose it to round off the *Symphonie* and invalidate its pessimistic title. Overcurious listeners asked: "Where did you drag up that extraordinary noise like a sawmill?" They would have been very surprised by the revelation that Pierre Henry had extracted it, with a grimace of pleasure, from the delicate E string of a violin.

7

Our actions follow us. Red labels. Important indications.
Should we envy men of other ages? Fissures of randomness.
Congratulations and red tape. Future plans. A classical
epilogue. A Greek philosopher beside a concrete sea.

A new international conference, this time in Italy, was to keep me from the studio again, and for a fairly long time. On my previous absences, I had put the key under the door cheerfully, without thinking about my return. But the situation had changed. Our actions—and all the more if they are concrete actions—follow us. My research had become firmly established, and I was no longer alone.

Pierre Henry had abandoned his kettledrums and was giving all his time to the studio. Within a few months he had acquired skills in manipulation that amazed even sound engineers. His wife, who came at first out of curiosity, then as a voluntary assistant, was soon changed into the mistress of the house. It was none too soon. The proliferation of objects required cupboards, tidying, filing. Michèle Henry took charge of the cupboards with authority, energy, and kindliness. Within a few months the ancient boxes where I stacked the records from number 2002 to 5997 had given way to filing cabinets where green, red, blue, and yellow labels executed an initial classification. The system of colored labels had been made fashionable by Maurice Le Roux. In other words, we were beginning to set up shop and I had to go away again. How could we consolidate our position during my absence?

There was, of course, radio. Paris-Inter had broadcast the *Suite* 14 in 1949 without any noteworthy reactions. What is more, concrete music was not intended only for radio. As this was a musical experiment, we had to play the game to the bitter end, stop broadcasting, and risk the adventure of a concert hall performance. It seemed difficult to carry out this plan before I left for Italy. Two invitations anticipated our wishes. One came from the Triptyque, suggesting the hall in the Ecole Normale de Musique for a first concert on March 18; the other was from the Sorbonne Groupe de Philosophie, offering the Richelieu amphitheater for a conference. Raymond Bayer was to introduce us at the Sorbonne, and Serge Moreux at the Triptyque. On the invitation was a quotation, a little text by Serge Moreux, much too complimentary for my taste and which—with his permission—I have soft-pedaled a bit: "There are important moments in the birth of the arts: taking part in them is not always pleasant. The first real concert of concrete music is one of these moments. Listening to Pierre Schaeffer's musical scores has nothing to do with musical civility, puerile and honest. It is somewhat like discovering a sound continent as virgin as Robinson Crusoe's island. However arduous, these sorts of expeditions afford some pleasure . . . of the unforeseen at the very least." The program was in two parts: the "classical repertoire" and the first performance of the *Symphonie pour un homme seul,* in a—too-long—version with twenty-two sequences lasting forty-five minutes. Serge Moreux gave a speech, the gist of which was

> The material of concrete music is sound in its native state as provided by nature, fixed by machines, transformed by their manipulations.
>
> Between these fragments and those derived from them, there are no affective or acoustic relationships other than those that preside in the scattered and glittering physical universe.
>
> The space filled by concrete music is the space ruled over by the machine and what lies beyond it, that world of vibrations, colors, and vol-

umes unknown to our musicians' ears, still in thrall to all the mechanisms of music.

It is amazing that a man should wish to build works of the mind with these. Despite the many imperfections of their initial construction, they stand out with their own logic, their psyche at the limits of our own, their dialectic of the fortuitous.

There was a Middle Ages of stone: they carved it. There is a Middle Ages of sound waves: we capture them. The artist need not choose any other avant-garde. Between the byzantine interplay of syntaxes and the return to forgotten or dried-up sources, the modern musician can, in Pierre Schaeffer's words, try to find a breach in the wall of music that surrounds us like a fortress.

I was, myself, fairly ill at ease. I went over to a sort of desk in the front row of the stalls, which had on it the potentiometers of a mixer that controlled the sound in the concert hall. Jacques Poullin had installed the turntables on the stage between two loudspeakers. Thus we occupied, fairly recklessly, the magic circle where the usual sight is strings vibrating, bows susurrating, reeds palpitating under the inspired baton of the conductor. The audience had to be content with an infinitely more disappointing sight: turntables and potentiometers, cables and loudspeakers. Such were the objects we were obliged to display.

Jacques Poullin, who was busy "synchronizing" the records, was relatively relaxed. I, on the other hand, was troubled by contradictory feelings. Was I in charge or wasn't I? Should the loudspeaker volume be adjusted once and for all, or, following a vague intuition, should some sort of presence respond to the audience's presence, not leave it alone in front of the turntable, add a level of performance, however minimal, to the automatically produced recording? It was only after the event that I took stock of my legitimate boldness. I had indeed to be there, and, to however small an extent, (apparently), interpret. But I also had to put any regret behind me, not feel like a disillusioned conductor, and carry it off before a somewhat dazed audience, with no other means of expression than imperceptible hand movements that added to or reduced the general sound level by a few *decibels*.

I had revealed my difficulties in some paragraphs in the program. These indicated my anxiety. This concert had been too hastily prepared, I knew. It was, however, necessary not so much to show concrete music in performance as to direct future research. It was an experiment, and I accepted its results, positive or negative, in advance. But I couldn't get rid of some unease: insolence, usurpation. What harm was I doing to that respectable place in the first violins that my father had occupied for thirty years?

> Should we envy men from other ages, their laborious slowness, their complicity with time? Or should we glory in what we can do, engraving time on a piece of wax that holds all the sounds in the world but that the world hardly gives us time to examine, which we explore with the speed of Vandals and which we rush to display, not without secret shame, but with the apostolic fervor of the discoverer of continents?
>
> If atomic rhythm had not yet invaded the planet, if the works of modern humanity could be developed and pursued slowly and secretly in some Cartesian retreat, then indeed it would not have been necessary to perform this "concrete music" immediately, while scarcely out of limbo, full of technical imperfections and aesthetic uncertainties. But for us XXth-century men, our reflections are explosive, our laboratories are in the marketplace, our arts are machine-made, but this should be no cause for scandal. Who dares to throw the powerful tool aside because it is too new?

There followed a paragraph on rendering to Caesar that which was Caesar's:

Contemporary Industries need to offer fissures of randomness for the poetic adventure to slip through. There are not many of them. French Broadcasting occasionally lends itself to such breaking and entering. It is certainly the only one in the world. Thank God for it.

And it was very true that there were indeed not two radio stations in the world where the adventure of concrete music could have been born. I had traveled enough to know this.

The manifesto continued with an appeal:

> We have taken up the tool that technology gave us, we have not balked at the task, and the result, after all, is not entirely our work. The child of gods and men, of will and chance, it is a found and not entirely willed object that we are displaying to find out if it can be of use.
>
> The musician-engineer, once he has managed to extract something from the humming of machines, also has a right to be relieved of duty.

Let the ingenious musician take over. Not, of course, one who wants a prefabricated object. But one who would enjoy the material and that unexpected way of playing a multiple instrument, and who would give up his manuscript paper for the ever-changing hues of discs. Let someone like this come to the rescue if he wishes.

Despite the somewhat Gionesque lyricism of this passage, the appeal was to be for the moment in vain. As for the public, they were put on their guard with good reason:

And let the public not be too hasty in judgment, either for or against. First, they must listen again. Once is not enough. For us it is not so much a matter of expressing ourselves in front of an audience as of persuading them to consider the object. It is perhaps the object that has something to say to us.

This statement, which I always think is one of the most important, fell, like everything else, on astonished, but well-meaning, ears.

As for the press, it showed some sympathy for our endeavor. So Roger Richard wrote in *Combat* (July 19, 1950):

The performances already given at the Club d'Essai, or, last March, at the Ecole Normale de Musique, have proved that an audience, without being specially prepared or informed, coped very well with the shock of this unprecedented music . . . Concrete music is ready to come out of the laboratory. It is time for musicians to bring it out . . . The fact that musicians and musicologists such as Roland-Manuel, Olivier Messiaen, and Serge Moreux are showing interest gives us hope that this will be the case.

Serge Moreux, who had supported us with so much understanding, called the first true concert of concrete music a "historic event," and in the *France-Asie* review, in June 1950, René de Obaldia, who saw me as the devil incarnate, nevertheless added:

We must, however, mention here the extraordinary degree of pathos and tragedy that these first attempts involve us in. And with good reason. We are placed before the reproduction of that mechanical universe that has become our own, and that every day dominates us more. Pitiless testimony. The drama of our time is engraved on wax without honey.

And Clarendon, in *Figaro*, August 4, 1950:

Faced with the first experiments in concrete music, I would like to explain to readers who have asked me what it is all about and straightaway
give my personal feelings about what I have just read and heard. The idea
of a "concrete music" must have arisen from a pessimistic observation.
The language of music is evolving rapidly and equally rapidly wearing
out. We must constantly find new forms of expression, which, incidentally,
is less difficult than discovering a completely new way of thinking . . .
More seriously, let us say that we are, if not at the beginning of a true art,
at least at the birth of a procedure whose future and whose applications
it is still impossible to foresee.

In general, these different reactions echoed our own uncertainties.
One of our critics castigated us with the Chinese proverb: "Whatever
makes a noise does no good and whatever does good makes no noise."
But the Chinese, as well, make music . . . One thing, however, was certain. Concrete music existed. But to us it seemed premature to make
value judgments about it. Pure experimentation is morally neutral, and
it is only through the ways they are used that discoveries enter into the
world of values. Whatever the case, after the first concert we should have
preferred a real battle, one of those polemics that consolidate discoveries.
It is a strange time, and Paris a strange country, where everything possible is conceivable, where even scandal is immediately cross-faded onto
an understanding smile, and scornful or amused irony.

At the same time, some friends, including Maurice Le Roux, took
some of our records abroad with them and played them at international
gatherings, such as the one at Salzburg.

Independently of any fundamental debate on the principle of concrete music itself, the concert at the Ecole Normale de Musique demonstrated to us that no disservice was done to concrete music by recording
it on records or tape. But performing it in a concert hall presented several problems.

The first was purely technical. It was to ensure the best sound projection, by accommodating our equipment to the acoustics and size of the
hall, by installing our loudspeakers in the best places, and above all by
achieving a three-dimensional projection. We knew that by carrying out

more experiments we should eventually be able to work out valuable rules for the future, but for the moment we were only at the first attempt at a public concert, and this was not without trial and error, and great anxiety.

A second problem was human interaction with the machines. We had to give a little flick of the thumb to the potentiometers and create some interpretative space, however small, to facilitate contact with the public. What if the conductor, apart from the dynamics, were in charge of the three-dimensionality, if his gestures sketched out in space the trajectory that the sounds would make in the hall? Would not this, for the public, be the new performance mode, in which sound objects, although prefabricated, would appear dynamic and alive, once more part of the visible art of a performer?

And so new problems were added to the various problems we had already identified, such as the problems of the theory of concrete music and of instrumentation, with the result that the talk given some days previously at the Sorbonne was already out of date, and the field of our research extended.

Some days before I left, I was given an invitation by a mathematician friend who had been won over by the concert at the Ecole Normale. How could we help others to share what he had experienced? A rather skeptical philosopher was there too. After the analyst's speculations, the philosopher, a specialist in Greek philosophy and himself a Greek, asked if concrete music could rightly be called music . . . I explained my scruples to him myself. Classical music, it appears, abstracts forms from all matter. Concrete music, on the contrary, turns its back on these pure forms and, while it revitalizes matter, it also presents itself as a sort of huge deterioration. Greek philosophy was against me. For the Greek philosophers, everything deteriorates once it leaves the idea. For them, the tragedy of the world is to wrest the world from chaos. Saving the world means giving form, creating the existent snatched from nothingness. Hence this definition of music: "That which is wrested from time, yet made of time, but giving form to time." For example, said the philosopher, if, as has happened unforgettably to me, I listen to the sound of waves while sitting deep within a cave, is that music? I reply, yes, just about. Even if there is no musical work on the part of the object, is there not musical work by the subject in the very fact of extracting this sound element from its chaotic context, hence of drawing from it, subjectively, a form? It's yet another way, said the analyst, of rescuing time, and therefore of creating music . . . I expand on the subject: the concrete experiment in music consists in constructing sound objects, no longer from the interplay of numbers and metronomically marked seconds, but with pieces of time wrested from the cosmos. If, in the example of the cave, music just about exists, it is because, through an act of pure will, the subject takes the sound of the waves from external chaos into conscious order. So, for there to be music, all that is needed is that a relationship be established between subject and object, and the initial act in music is willed hearing, i.e., selecting from the chaotic hubbub of sounds a sound fragment that one has decided to consider. Here the memory acts as a closed groove: it retains, it records, it repeats. This fragment must be considered for all it contains: matter and form. It can be repeated, imitated, combined with others. Hence a subject could create a music for himself out of a continuous chaotic chain of sound by imposing externally a form that comes from within him, provided that he can go a little faster than external time, and, when he has scarcely started listening, is agile enough to hear, as if he were creating it himself, the emerging form that he is doing more than listen to: which he recognizes. Do we need to point out that the example of the waves, which allows me to compose an inner music, is not chosen altogether at random? In pure chaos, it is probably impossible to hear a music in its emergent state. The sound of waves is not chaos: there is rhythm and pulsation, and each wave is a variation on an immutable theme. By a fortunate chance, the Greek philosopher's example was too well chosen. Some time later, informed by further equally useful conversations, this time with physicists, I could have given him the key to the enigma, thanks to so-called "information" theories. If the noise of waves has a chance of being musical, it is because, like music, like every message, it is affected by *redundancy* . . .

PART II Second Journal
of Concrete Music

1950–1951

8

A happy homecoming. Sounds in every genre. Musics without title or score. Pierre and ambiguities. Theoretical preoccupations. All-or-nothing musicians. Wherein one loses one's tablature. A historic document: the Vth movement. Causal score and effects score.

Sometimes chemists and biologists can be overwhelmed by their precipitates and cultures. On my return, despite Michèle Henry's diligence, sound objects had mushroomed dangerously. Every system of classification had failed. It was the same with the works. Was Pierre Henry's extraordinary fecundity to be a source of regret? He had discovered in himself a sort of turntable genius. What's more, he had taken possession of a special machine that I had had built before I left, and which enabled discs to be recorded and made at variable speeds. In his hands the new machine had created extraordinary sound objects by the hundred: samples, sequences—what name could be given to the splinters of sound to which, sometimes, Pierre Henry managed to give a certain degree of sound development?

We began to have visitors, among them directors whose radio productions were very well adapted to our discoveries. When the scenario included a realistic noise, we could often, as the creator did with Adam's rib, fashion an initial sound element from this noise and then develop it. Neither sound effect nor symphony, concrete music easily demonstrated its dramatic effectiveness, its radiophonic interest. Our pretend airplanes, our imaginary cars, our synthetic cries were just surreal enough to put across the real in sounds that were sufficiently violent.

In response to demand, but without his work being permanently interrupted, Pierre Henry had composed a repertoire whose three series, *Péripéties* (Incidents), *Climats* (Climates), and *Ponctuations* (Punctuations), gave directors a variety of resources, going from "panic" to "cyclone" for *Incidents;* from "mad roundabout" to "night flight" for *Climats,* and from "the curtain rises" to "accelerating motorbike" for *Ponctuations.*

The table of posing times, which haunts the first efforts of amateur photographers, is not unlike this list: white clouds, ships at sea . . . groups under thick foliage. This list, for which I have always felt warm affection, would have saved us using our imagination. It would have done just as well as "Night Flight" or "Cottage Industry," whose perfectly interchangeable tracks could have been used in a scenario to the glory of Agriculture or Aviation, respectively.

In reality the problem of names remained a major one. We encountered it when giving titles to the short sequences of about one minute, which we offered to broadcasters. Nor would the fragments, which constituted our experimental material for sound objects, be described with any adequate qualifier.

But music does very well without words, at least for a time. It can even do completely without signs, and thus without a score. How, during my absence, had Pierre Henry managed to compose two important works, a *Concerto des ambiguïtés* (Concerto of ambiguities) and a *Suite* so difficult to name that only the title "Untitled Music" could be allotted to it? One question alone would have embarrassed him, the question of writing the scores for them.

There were plenty of fragments of initial scores. In the *Concerto des ambiguïtés* the characteristic phrases were notated musically (fig. 10); on the contrary, cinema-style continuity editing was used for Untitled Music.

But once they had been played on the prepared piano, then manipulated, these elements had become unrecognizable. And so we had to at-

FIGURE 10. [Initial element of a fragment of *Concerto des ambiguïtés.*]

tack the finished work head on and try to capture the orchestration resulting from it. If, in fact, some piano sounds were heard as coming from a celeste or a set of kettledrums, we had to distinguish between the instrument as means and the instrument as result.

The score presented two problems of principle: tablature and notation technique. In vain we summoned the best professional musicians to the rescue. However crowned with honors they were, they jibbed at a problem that was unusual more than insoluble and focused their attention on the hectic work of musical decoding. It was no good my repeating that we couldn't notate everything, or, at this point, fit the sound objects that appeared randomly into a theoretical system: they balked at the leap, and in their obstinate insistence on rigorously notating everything, they declared themselves incapable of notating anything at all. I told them to make it simpler and bring out what I called the "large notes." For example, the last movement of the *Concerto* presented an extraordinary tangle of sounds in an outlandish tempo yet finally resolved on a huge final note, repeated three times, more and more loudly, as if the aim of the entire work had been simply to prepare for the bursting forth of a pure note. But for them this note did not stand out, as they were so used to considering all notes as equal, to "playing the notes," as they say. If only they had had about them something of the physicist, for in their conservatoires they learn to distinguish between orders of magnitude! Because everywhere in concrete music it was evident that a great quantity of rhythmical musical figures or patterns in tessitura needed to be organized into a hierarchy. The only way out of the problem of notation was to organize musical values into a hierarchy. Because we had not only to organize into hierarchies, but to differentiate. The principle of notation had to be variable. Some elements should be notated with the greatest precision, some intervals to a vanishing point and some rhythms to a tenth of a second. At other times we had to be content with an approximate outline: variations extended in tessitura but with vague, irrational rhythms, yet with a comprehensible overall development. If the sound complex were particularly hermetic, if, although recognizable to the ear, it were far too difficult to analyze, it could be represented by a symbol and referenced by a letter. At least it was possible to distinguish a series of unrelated incidental elements and designate them by the signs I^1, I^2, I^3, or, on the other hand, a sound object recognizable across its variations (or more precisely in all its variety), and represent it by the letters A^1, A^2, A^3. Such a simple set of symbols was more likely to lead to a score than scrupulous notations with no connection with the articulation of the objects (fig. 11).

The problem of tablature, apparently simpler than notation, raises even thornier questions of principle. We noticed that instrumental notation in music was defined only by the situation. There were two violins, a viola, and a cello, and that was enough for the strings to be represented by four parallel staves. But if no causal clue enabled the instruments to be identified, how, when listening to a musical ensemble, could pseudoinstruments be discovered and defined? Should we, for example, align the staves from top to bottom according to the layout of the material, i.e., mainly the timbres? And what if, during a sound arabesque, the material were to change two or three times? Should we align the list of objects, A, B, C, vertically if it were in a score where the identity of these objects

	(1)			(2)
staves 1 and 2 (incidental motifs)		I^1	I^2	I^3 :
staves 2 and 3 (varying motifs)	A^1	A^2	A^3	

FIGURE 11. Symbolic reduction of bar 1 of *Prosopopée I* (see fig. 9).

stood out strongly? Would this be to admit that, instead of developing horizontally in time, the element of form was involved in the vertical arrangement that until then had been reserved for the means? Great was our embarrassment. This problem would probably remain with us for a long time.

Finally I got my colleagues to adopt the principle of a provisional tablature, inspired by classical orchestral tablature, where the four voices and strings are set out separately, one at the top and the other at the bottom of the page. The rest of the orchestra, wind instruments and percussion instruments, is in two other sets of staves, while the keyboard instruments are judiciously posted on the frontier of the percussion and continuous sounds. Seen from a concrete point of view, the classical score already takes into account the most and the least living (voices as opposed to instruments) and the most and the least musical (strings as opposed to percussion). The first criterion could be this: Is there or is there not a live presence perceived behind the sounds? The other question was: Are the sounds perceived more, or less, musical? Do they, like percussion, have a significant element of noise, or, like wind instruments, a more significant melodic element?

So, by analogy with the four groups of classical tablature (voice, wind, percussion, strings), it was possible to distinguish: first, the group of living elements; second, prepared instruments; third, noises; and fourth, the classical orchestra. The analogy could be explained as follows: the living elements, the voices, unambiguously demonstrate the presence of life; the orchestra responds to the voices through the permanence of a pure musical element. The noise and the prepared instrument groups share the space available between the musical and the organic. The noises move away from the musical organization and the prepared instruments

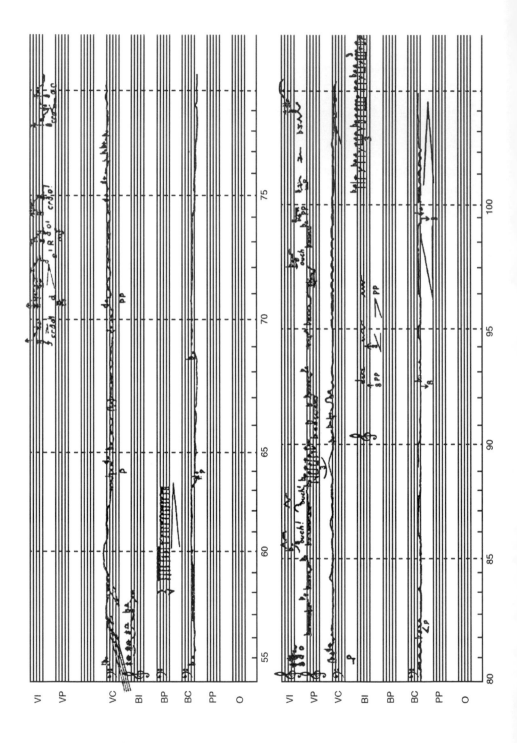

move closer to it (the term *prepared* refers to tricks used with ordinary instruments to produce different sound effects from when they are played). The two groups at the bottom of the page came into the category of traditional musical notation; the two groups of living elements and of noises were usually notated by symbols and graphics. They in turn were divided into three subgroups:

- so-called incidental elements (if they followed each other without repetition)
- reiterated elements
- evolving elements

A conclusive experiment was carried out on the fifth movement of Pierre Henry's *Musique sans titre* (Untitled music [fig. 12]). Five of us took the three-minute record home with us and for many long hours tried to decode and notate it as best we could. In fact, our notations did not contradict but complemented each other. Each pair of ears had come to different conclusions about different elements of the analysis. Maurice Le Roux made the synthesis, and some details were revised by Yvette Grimaud.

Writing this score was a decisive, and more richly informative, step than many experiments. We had been forced to reflect on concrete music and to consider whether a concrete orchestra really existed. It was still only a step on the way. We understood later that, in some cases, we had to go so far as to give up the notion of an orchestra. That this notion was tied to the idea of a music with a fixed, tangible structure and formal development. While the trumpet, the strings, etc., are invariants of matter, musical development is formal and will appear on the several lines

---

FIGURE 12 *(opposite)*. [First experimental score for concrete music *(Musique sans titre)*.]

"Voice" group: VI, incidental voice (human or animal); VP, periodic voice (vocal element); VC, continuous voice (vocal element).
"Noise" group: BI, incidental noise; BP, periodic noise; BC, continuous noise.
"Prepared instruments" group: PP, prepared piano.
"Ordinary instruments" group: O, orchestral instruments.

FIGURE 13. [Examples of causal score and effects score (eighteenth century).]

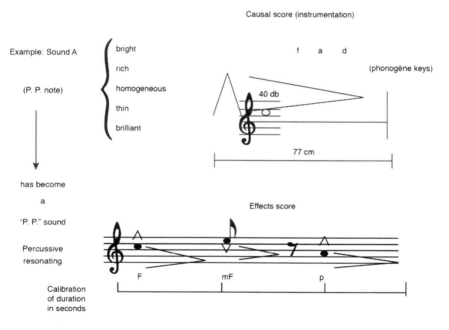

FIGURE 14. [Same example in concrete music.]

of the score, each of which refers to one of these instrumental invariants. If the trumpet is cross-faded with the violin, if, for example, there is a Schönbergian *Klangfarbenmelodie* on a sustained note, we no longer have a horizontal and vertical grid. There is interpenetration of both matter and form. But as trumpet and strings are recognizable and referable, the score can still take the classical form, provided it is clearly recognized that the horizontal-vertical element no longer corresponds to the harmony-counterpoint distinction. For a simple melodic notation the two vertical and horizontal coordinates on the score must be used. If there is no instrumental point of reference, form and matter can no longer be discerned; a horizontal line can, at best, only represent a melody, or more precisely a monophony, and in this monophony, form and matter are very closely linked. This is still an "effects" score, where the analysis of a polyphony would appear through contrasts between horizontal lines that depict associated monophonies. We have to set against—and, occasionally, for practical reasons choose in preference to—this "effects" score an "operational" score, a register that shows, in relation to the passage of time, all the operations needed to obtain effects that the ear can perceive and appreciate, but which, at the present moment, it is impossible to represent accurately with appropriate symbols (fig. 14). Incidentally, this is a classic distinction in ancient music (fig. 13).

9

In which we decide to keep a diary. On the difficulty of getting started. Orphée (Orpheus), or the wind in the treetops. In which we seriously consider a concrete opera. First stumbling blocks. Generalization of melody.

1951. April 1. Today I have decided to write down everything pertaining to the composition of a new work of concrete music, *Orphée,* in order to provide essential pointers in my research for possible successors.

Maurice Le Roux, whom I met yesterday, is standing down. He needs all his time for his own work. I am sorry he will not be taking part, but his objections were holding us back. They would only have been helpful if he had spent the same amount of time as us on research—at the point where it is—the same attention, and a commitment similar to that which unites Pierre Henry and me.

April 2. Since I have decided to make scrupulous notes in this diary on everything that might enlighten anyone who later finds himself in the same situation as us, this is the time to mention our discomfiture. We want to create a work. How shall we go about it? First, provide ourselves with material, then trust to instinct? And how shall we establish the score? How are we to imagine a priori the thousand unexpected transformations of concrete sound? How can we choose between hundreds of samples when no system of classification, and no notation, has yet been decided upon?

My efforts over previous years have always seen the light after a period of retreat. I was in the Alps, for winter sports, when I thought out the *Symphonie pour un homme seul.* I am relying on my next holiday in the Alps to think about *Orphée.*

April 3. The note, the key, the stave are so suited to classical music that it is possible to mistake the score for the work. It is its exact blueprint. Champions of the abstract say that it is the work itself. Ansermet says,[1] quite paradoxically, that the work is always beyond what is written down; Toscanini, if I remember aright, and a large number of honest-to-goodness musicians maintain that all one needs to do is play what is written. Personally, I agree with this. In any case, it doesn't matter very much. But there is a great gulf between baroque instrumental resources, the sketchy scores of concrete music, and the psycho-physiological impact it has on the audience. One is caught between fear of mystifying and the dread of mystery. A movement of the bow responds with dignity to the composer's notations, to the conductor's baton. But the effects of a turn of a handle on the gramophone, an adjustment of the potentiometer, are unpredictable—or at least we can't predict them yet. And so we reel dizzily between fumbling manipulations and erratic effects, going from the banal to the bizarre. It is outrageous. And from now on, it is this outrageousness that we must take on.

April 4. I am in a state of alert, hoping to find materials to fill these great gaps, hints of a method. Even the idea of *Orphée* is a throwing down of the gauntlet. Suffering horribly from the discordance of concrete music

---

1. Ernest Ansermet, *L'expérience musicale et le monde d'aujourd'hui* (Musical experience and today's world), Rencontres internationales de Genève (Neuchâtel: La Baconnière, 1948).

and also from its inhumanity, I am seeking a test of strength. *Orphée* has always been the triumph of the human lyre, the power given over Hell. If the musician is punished in love, his art at least has triumphed over the gods. Never mind the history of this couple; the real subject is the lone man, a divided Orpheus, with Eurydice (according to tradition as well) only an obscure bit player.

Where did the probably absurd idea of an *Orphée* come from? From seeing Maria Ferès in Gluck. Beyond the white-painted face crowned with black hair, sexless, mediated by that amazing voice, not at all "operatic," a personal adventure, both private and universal, was being played out, a solitude, a readiness for anything that flouted the world and society. A heroine at the Champs-Elysées, Maria Ferès occasioned boldness, was an example of recklessness. Opposite a contralto Orpheus, Eurydice should be an actress, a Maria Casarès, for example. Extraordinary duets: spoken against sung voice, bel canto against concrete orchestra. Autoduets: I imagine Orpheus singing with his own voice; as for Eurydice, she creates a hell of words that is her hell. Speech traps a being in her own thoughts. The hell of noise is not the worst. Everyone hides their own hell deep within their own existence, with no way out.

April 7—Courchevel. I've spent a long time thinking about the work as a whole, and even before planning its musical structure, I am inclined to create a scenario.

First, ideas. Or, in cinema parlance, visual effects: the tearing of Orpheus's veil, an excessively slow tearing, giving rise to a noise that forms the main constituent of one of the sequences. At first I put it at the beginning, then I keep it for the end. I imagine hands as well. Behind a wall, where Eurydice is hiding, hang (plaster of paris) hands, and Orpheus has to recognise Eurydice's. But it is very likely that the work will not follow this initial plan—even if I manage to come up with it a priori. When I imagined an organic Symphony of man, man descending into himself, I had imagined little people going down through the stomach and duodenum on ropes and ladders. What was left of this first idea? From the start, sounds of a crowd had erupted; even the cave noises had worked their way toward the light. How annoying for me, that the Symphony had moved so far from the original scenario! Would it be the same with *Orphée?* This time I determine to carry out my plan rigorously. But secretly I'm relying on the "blessings" of the studio.

1951. April 8. How can I describe the anguish, the bitter disappointment, at times the fury, that accompanies the genesis of a new work of concrete music? Where shall I start? Two radically opposed approaches are possible: either take a Scarlatti sonata, as we did some days ago, and transpose it note by note, or look for similarities of form. But this doesn't give good results, because inappropriate material is being subjected a priori to a framework that was not made for it. Or else go into the studio, play some records, and repeat the experiments with rolling tin cans. Should we continue to follow the whim of the elements if they are clearly the strongest? Those who give advice do not have to foot the bill. It's no good telling us to define our vocabulary, our symbolism; are the sound elements that we have discovered words that can be put into sentences? Western music, with its arithmetical base, is indeed a language, a form of speech. The composer expresses ideas, develops them, and concludes. There is nothing like this in concrete music. From here on, can concrete music hang together, and how can it be made to develop?

People always come back to two ways of making links, depending on whether they establish relationships of form or of matter. In a "concrete melody" (all the more forgiving for being more ample), nothing prevents the most disparate elements from being linked together with the greatest continuity: noise developing into musical sound, which then changes into human voice, and can change back into noise. Continuity of matter applies not only to matter itself but to rhythm as well. Little by little, by small shifts in continuity, a rhythm takes shape. At first it will be perceived as a vibration of the matter; then its shifts become more marked until continuity suddenly appears. So a form can come from matter. This continuity, which I can imagine, is already completely different from:

1. the cyclic character of the first concrete studies, through the repetition of the same fragment
2. serialist tendencies (illustrated, for example, by the first sequence of the *Symphonie pour un homme seul*)

Melody did indeed exist in this *Prosopopée*, but it was composed of collages: blows, cries, applause, sequences on the prepared piano. Rather than a melody, it was a series of volumes or values situated in an architectural work or a cubist painting. Whereas the continuity that I am seeking would signal a return to musical expression.

10

The record that can't be found. A chemist of good will. Botanics
of sound. In which wires get crossed and the mood deteriorates.
On the difficulty of training colleagues. The new equipment.

April 12. Back to Paris. Unfruitful session in the studio, where I am trying to get my colleagues to help me find elements for *Orphée*. Everyone is
focusing on the analytical files, which I have already mentioned. But, as
in any collection, there is an abundance of common varieties, and the
rare species is lacking. The green records have proliferated in directions
that are far too vague; the red ones are more interesting, and are accu-
mulating finds that are already expressive. Oh well, you don't always get
what you want. So where shall I find that sudden intake of breath, which
I have already heard, and which I need for *Orphée?* The irony of the situation: explanations, onomatopoeias, nothing helps me to get Pierre
Henry to identify it, though he is responsible for this magic gulp.

April 14. Today I received a letter from a listener: ". . . I wonder—and I
am doubtless not the first—if it would be possible, and, if so, useful, to

set up a chemistry of sounds, based on natural chemistry, i.e., to classify sounds into simple and compound elements, and to draw up a classification like Mendeleev's, etc. . . . What do you think?" —M. F.

This letter is opportune. Unfortunately, our problems won't be solved by chemistry. Mendeleev's table already exists in music; it's the table of powers of the number two. It's very clear that the field of composite sounds that we're developing could not possibly benefit from such a simple classification. The notion of organic chemistry is perhaps more interesting insofar as it classifies bodies according to function and not composition; modern chemistry is researching into formulas for nitrogen, oxygen, hydrogen, carbon . . . The interest lies in reducing complex organic compounds to elements that are just as complex but known and already classified. It's more likely that we'll have to adopt a botanical type of classification. It would have the virtue of creating order, even if it is based only on distinguishing features.

April 15. A strange labyrinthine period. In the studio cellars Jacques Poullin is unraveling the network of tangled wires belonging to the "potentiomètre d'espace" (space potentiometer). This is a new creation, for which we have great hopes, and which should enable us to re-create the gestures of an orchestral conductor. With his left hand he will control the fine detail, and with his right he will be able to influence the trajectory of the sounds in the concert hall. Jacques is also trying out new "shell-shaped speakers" in the Erard hall. As for the studio, it's in a total mess. The floorboards have holes in them to let cables through. There could not be more clutter. Nevertheless, in the space of a few months our equipment has made great strides. But the problem of concrete music will not necessarily be eased by this. It could even be that this technical development will muddy the waters even more.

April 16. The notorious record "sudden intake of breath" has been found. This human—so inhuman—breath is based on a rolling tin can. Pierre Henry, who has the secret, came across it when he was sorting some records looking for elements for *Orphée* to give to me. A happy day: several other "high-tension" sound fragments, among them a "snatch of jazz," again a product of Pierre Henry's irreplaceable talent. How is it done? By mingling two jazz records, he says, and taking extracts "ripped out with the cross-switch." There is still something spasmodic left over from the jazz, but there is now a huge, dramatic intake of breath as well.

So our attempts to systematize are coming up against the facts. To try and replace talent, skill, and chance combined with intuition too soon with theory would be to kill the goose that laid the golden egg. It's better to aim for the troubadours than Tannhäuser. I thank God for putting Pierre Henry on the road to the studio. Right from his second session in the studio he was on the ball with concrete music. This sort of guy never asks for explanation, and he gets to work right where the work is at.

April 18. Duhamel, whom I meet in the corridor every day, is very keen on being associated with concrete music. Faced with a request like this, I always feel torn between the desire to say yes and the fear of having too many on the team.

This gives me the opportunity to draft out, for future reference, the role of any new colleagues in concrete music:

1. amateurs: they will come from time to time, listen, and discuss.
2. "associates" (broadcasters, cinema, or theater directors) will use concrete music without making it themselves.
3. trainees: after a period of instruction (when will we be able to define this?), they will participate in our work. Their future will depend on their gifts for concrete music, our budget, the availability of studio funds.

April 19. I am thinking about the concrete orchestra and I believe I have discovered a fundamental law about it. I have chosen a certain number of "fragments" for *Orphée,* in which form and matter are interwoven. But these fragments are the starting point for transformations. If, in the course of these transformations, there is a certain "unvaryingness" of the initial fragment, it will play the part of a pseudoinstrument. It will appear vertically in the tablature of the concrete orchestra. So what are the criteria of unvaryingness? Some sounds, for example, have sliding, snatched, or "flaring" (i.e., going rapidly from piano to forte) attacks. If these characteristics remain throughout the modulations that the sounds undergo, then we have sound sources that can play the part of orchestral instruments. Thus the following laws could be extrapolated:

1. an orchestral element (pseudoinstrument) is identified by the permanence of one characteristic across different forms.

2. musical forms, significant or not, are achieved through development in time or the superimposition, at a given moment, of pseudoinstruments. This development may affect all the characteristic elements of a given matter (tessitura, dynamic, timbre, note structure, even criterion of structure itself) except at least one, which remains *unvarying* and consequently marks out the identity of the orchestral element to which the form applies.

3. instrumental techniques, or performance procedures, involve a range of activities, recognizable or not to the ear, and it is important to distinguish their causal, or operational, character. Only the effect is important to the ear.

So there are two types of score: the operative score, a sort of directions for use, and the effects score, which develops along parallel lines the forms taken by each of the elements of the orchestra[1] and which alone can give an idea of the structure of a work.

April 21. For some days I have been going around with the first page of my score. Various reactions from my colleagues. Pierre Henry finds it too precise. It isn't precise enough for Micheline Banzet. Pierre is very suspicious of signs that are so unconcrete: notes and staves. I know he will always go his own way. Micheline, on the contrary, hates vague notation and would rejoice at the thought of finally playing real notes with real flats and real naturals . . . But in any case, no one really knows how to play our instruments yet!

April 22. I am drafting out a theory on paper. The need to write down makes us focus our ideas. The concepts of "fragment and "element" emerge

---

1. This only applies to one type of music, where the concept of pseudoinstrument is valid. There is a whole type of music where the concept of pseudoinstrument no longer applies.

from the test victorious. The classification of sound objects comes out less so. At least a dozen parameters must be involved, and I don't quite know how to choose them. If I had them, I would hold the key to that characterology that would branch out and connect up with genres, species, varieties . . .

April 23. Time is short, as we have to prepare a demonstration for the end of the year, and our final research budget depends directly on this. Work in the studio has held us back. I must accept that, for both technical and aesthetic reasons, I won't be able to create *Orphée* from wholly new elements, as I would have wished. Technically, I would have liked very bright elements, with no background noise, which could be modulated in many ways; aesthetically, I would have liked to make a new start, choose interesting matter, representing pseudoinstruments, which would have allowed us to write a score in advance. In effect, that would require many months of work—which we haven't got—and new trial and error. Every time we start work on live sound for example, we get quite primitive products that are not as good as those on the several thousand records that fill our cupboards. So, having explained the original scenario for *Orphée* to him, I am asking Pierre Henry, with the help of the index cards for all our records, to find elements that could provide materials, or even sequences, that could be used in the work just as they are. It will become more of a dramatic work, a display of juxtaposed samples. But can we do any better? The trawl through the records gives abundant and rich results. But I have to say that, for the sake of productivity, I am obliged to abandon my plans for a preestablished score. Pierre Henry rejoices. Micheline Banzet purses her lips.

April 24. General bad temper in the studio. I am at the end of my tether. On the pretext that the tape recorders are a special kind, ventilators, which are the rule in ordinary tape recorders, have been forgotten. Whose fault is it? These prototypes are provided through the good will of several services that have neither the time nor the means to supervise every detail of their workings. Four hours go by with all sorts of breakdowns and our tempers get worse. We busy ourselves with ventilators, control problems, late papers, impossible timetables, financial difficulties . . . and also next Sunday's broadcast, which we promised Paris IV and which we're not at all pleased with. Is this studio built on wishful thinking? I wonder if my stubbornness isn't madness.

April 25. I am continuing the search for material with Pierre Henry. At each session I use mnemonic titles to note down the passages I have heard: the green record 219 is called "Debussy." The striped green 313 bears the name "Back-to-Front Partita." Another is baptized "Subterranean Element." We also have a series of "Splashes" and a most engaging "Manifold." At last we are sorting through systematically, weeding out from the interesting elements anything that is technically poor. Finally we are making copies of them all to keep the originals intact.

April 27. I am starting some quite satisfying work with the copies I made yesterday and took back home. I'm making a jigsaw puzzle, identifying the different sound fragments for various passages of *Orphée*. Nevertheless, I won't use the records as they stand. I'll take only a few grooves here and there. It's the material that interests me. Of course, I haven't got nearly enough records for my puzzle, and as for unity of style, I'm already kissing it good-bye.

April 28. The wiring for the new equipment, including the *"phonogène,"* is scarcely finished. A difficult running-in period: it breaks down every time we use it. Sick of breakdowns, I go and join Micheline and Duhamel, who are trying their hand at analysis.

I find my two musicians abstracted in front of a page covered with double naturals and quarter-sharps. They are, of course, exhausted. In vain I suggest that scrupulously melodic and harmonic notation is not, for the time being, as important as they think, that the interest of analysis lies elsewhere . . . We're not talking about the same notes . . .

April 29. Interview at Jean Tardieu's with the representatives of the R.A.I. [Italian Radio Broadcasting], among them G. B. Angioletti, who runs literary programs on the R.A.I. We talk about Marinetti's movement. Russolo was the group's musician. There was also the painter Depero. It was

Russolo who invented the *intonarumori*. What exactly was this instrument? A sort of prepared piano? Or something like my first noise organ? Angioletti doesn't know.

When I go down to the studio again, I find my experts in prose translation still beavering away in front of their record.

April 30. The studio is a battlefield. Everyone—Jacques Poullin, Giaccobi, Pouedras—is fighting against the new equipment. Bristling with all sorts of defenses, the three-track tape recorder temporarily refuses to produce counterpoints. Once again I realize the infinite patience concrete music requires, especially when tape recorders are used. Although certainly preferable to records for several reasons, they are more delicate and take longer to manipulate. Would their resistance to manipulation, however, perhaps be a safeguard for the operator in the future? Because the dangerous facility with which we perform these manipulations on records (much loved by Pierre Henry particularly) would have to be disciplined!

11

Theory of Musical Repression. The Mystery of the octave. The beauty of the A. Gestalttheorie. *Humiliations and humility.* Orphée *in a coma. The author in Hell.*

May 1. Bad conscience theme. One of the oldest themes in concrete music, which I have carefully noted from the beginning of this journal when I first came to the studio (with the noise organ). Awareness of a sort of breaking of the rules, poor use of means toward an end that I should have attained directly. If, when I come out harassed from a session in the studio, I go to a concert, or if I sit down at the piano, "real" music seems like the repose of the blessed after the contortions of damnation.

Some young people from the generation after me are perfectly happy with these chaotic performances (Artaud, Dubuffet . . .). I, on the contrary, am fanatical about order. And how I miss it! I strive for it as for a sovereign good, which is refused, or frugally meted out, to me!

May 2. Why do we always do the opposite of what we like doing? Because, unable to achieve it fully, we try to attain it through indirect, ambiguous means. Why, when genius reveals itself, does it often do so in undesirable beings? Would it not be possible to explain a great painter, a great poet, by a certain inability to paint or to write? Ah! The others are missing something, taste, ideas, a secret that I alone have. What an artist, said Nero, dies with me! And yet it's too late for me to go into the Conservatoire. I still have the studio, where I do my teaching as an inventor.

And this could explain the (perhaps regrettable) discovery of concrete music, a sort of musical repression.

May 3. Conversation with friends about concrete music. Some people are "against" it, I can tell. Their reasons are rooted deep in their being and I sense it simply by the tactfulness of their faces, the cautiousness of their gestures. They are against concrete music inasmuch as they don't think with their hands. In the keen intelligences of the cautious, I can immediately see all the qualities I lack. Also, their faults are of the sort that I am armed against. Overall, I lose the first round against them. I had, for example, quite naïvely embroiled myself in the subject-object system as it applies to music. In my interlocutor's vocabulary, the words "subject" and "object" are no longer in use. He has definitively classified music as a language. I object that this anthropomorphism of language does not apply to concrete music. No, he says, music is a language, and anthropomorphism is the norm. I explain that the manipulations of concrete music create an objective music, which we still have to decipher. He thinks that concrete music is simply a branch of musical acoustics. In the same way, phonetics is not all there is to the study of language, only semantics can provide this.

As he speaks I can feel, as if it were quivering in my memory, the whole drama of these last three years of experimentation, when, in effect, I had to wrench fragments for the new language from acoustics. I know all too well that there is no musical phenomenon without acoustic manipulations, ingenious montages, the moment when it begins to "mean" something.

But the miracle of concrete music, which I am trying to get across to my interlocutor, is that, in the course of experimentation, things begin to speak by themselves, as if they were bringing a message from a world unknown to us and outside us. Initially the twelve notes of the scale were themselves a pure thing. Using these notes has turned them into a language. If I gather together fragments of noise, animal cries, the modulated sound of machines, I also am striving to articulate them like the words of a language, which I speak without even understanding it or ever having learned it; I am deciphering hieroglyphics. Does the difficulty of this conversation come from the fact that my interlocutor doesn't have the same confidence as I in the secret correspondence between man and the world, to which music is one of the keys? I attempt to sound him out on this: "Are you not surprised," I say to him, "that the perception of an octave and a fifth demonstrates our taste for simple relationships, makes us emotionally sensitive to the number 2, and the relationship 3/2 . . . Could you not conceive that this is a different phenomenon from language, since it is not concerned with signs or meaning? The octave and the fifth are not used to say something. Now, this is where man and the world come together, i.e., the manifestation in sound of numbers or fractions finds a direct resonance in the human heart. Isn't there something miraculous in this correspondence between subject and object?" My interlocutor then points out that it's the same in language in its broadest sense, that, for example, language can be reduced to two fundamental triangles, the *vocalic triangle* and the *consonantal triangle:* Ah, Oo, Ee, on the one hand, and, on the other, P, T, K. Like Monsieur Jourdain, I discover in my first phonetics lesson the three fundamental vowels and the three fundamental consonants. I immediately account for them by the use of the lips, the tongue, and the larynx. But I am not at all lost in admiration. I remark that this is, in effect, an analysis of the most general characters of the human phonatory organs, as if, for example, we were studying the timbre and the attack of an oboe reed or a horn. But there is no connection between this analysis of language and my suggestion, which, for the fraction 3/2 to correspond to the musical concept of the dominant, demands admiration for a correspondence between arithmetic and human sensibility.

My interlocutor refuses to see an objective relationship here, unless I allow—and he is prepared to reciprocate—that there is an objective element in all the sciences.

I would like to confound this stubborn fellow by asking him if, across the entire human race, a given vowel or diphthong has an objective concept associated with it. Do all *ahs* sound joyful? Or all *oohs* sad? If so, I would say that there are elements in language that link, if not men to the world, then men to each other, and that there is mystery, connectedness, between subject and object.

And furthermore, if this were the case, we should have to go back to the sources of language and to the causes of this secret relationship that makes all *ahs* joyful and all *oohs* sad. Clearly *ah* and *ooh* are fixed musical functions, and it is again through music that these elements of objectivity can be explained.

The conversation comes to a sudden end through mutual weariness. However, we agree on one point: musical theory is centuries out of date, for the theoreticians of "note by note" are like the grammarians, completely occupied with word for word. Nothing has yet been done with regard to the analysis of structures and forms, whether written into the musical works themselves or felt by the subject as general psycho-aesthetic behaviors that lend themselves to experimentation and understanding.

May 4. An example of the study of forms for a disinterested inquirer about music on the structures A and B (fig. 15).

1. What sort of objective relationship is there between these two forms (symmetry with relation to *D*)?

2. Do these forms have a psycho-aesthetic effect? Why?

3. Incidentally, is there an objective difference between the ordering of forms A B that is more satisfying than B A?

As may be expected, these questions are not answered in the musical sciences. As for *Gestalt*, it replies, like Molière's doctor, "Good health is profoundly significant." Ooh. Nothing but fine phrases . . .

May 5. Nothing this week. No time. It's been a week of wasted time, failures, exhaustion.

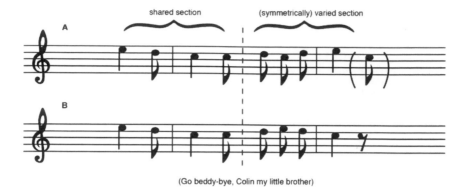

shared section   (symmetrically) varied section

A

B

(Go beddy-bye, Colin my little brother)

FIGURE 15. [Little example illustrating *Gestalttheorie*.]

May 7. As soon as I come into the studio, a sort of nausea takes hold of me. Vast amounts of material, and extreme difficulty in either linking it together or making it develop. I was relying on the new equipment. Although it was delivered in record time, it is far from being fit for our purpose. The twelve-note tape recorder emits extraneous clunks; the three-track tape recorder is extremely heavy to manipulate; the one with a slider is not set up. We're reduced to using the turntable again. Only Pierre Henry is comfortable in his instinctive technique. For the time being it's the only one that's productive, and I would hesitate to put pressure on him to abandon it. He has undeniably acquired a taste for concrete matter, and, not without bias, still makes very great demands on himself.

May 10. I went to the private viewing of the exhibition "May" at the Palais de Tokyo. How could I not be struck, yet again, by the similarity between concrete music and modern painting? For a long time now, no one has been shocked, when looking at paintings, by the absence of a subject, because paintings do not tell a story any more than they describe a landscape or a still life. The most interesting canvases are those where the formal element is so discreet, so simplified, that an impression of beauty emanates from them. Which leads to the thought that the most worthwhile pieces in concrete music are those that, far from seeking musical expression in the classical sense, illustrate simple form, beautiful matter; there's no need to look for an exposition, movements, details.

Denise C., who is giving a talk, tells me that she was at the first concrete music concert at the Ecole Normale de Musique and that it was the first musical experience that had ever moved her. Until then she had only been to concerts unwillingly and didn't enjoy any type of music.

May 11. The presence of my colleagues in the studio often weighs me down. It increases my sense of powerlessness. There is a certain ambition on my part to want to react against Pierre Henry's methods and introduce new ones, for Maurice Jarre, for example, who is beginning a period of training. Once more, my labor seems to me to be the result of absurd obstinacy. Why go on? The hours spent in the studio are for me so much time for writing that I haven't got. Today I forced myself to stay in the studio right to the end, already certain that I would achieve nothing. Giaccobi, always so endearing and sensitive behind his abrupt manners, understands the situation so well that he begins to give me his ideas: an orchestral chord, then a woman's voice . . . I am more humiliated with the technicians than with Jarre. I don't want to give them the impression, with all my ramblings, that I am making a mess of my work and wasting their time. Pierre Henry admits that he feels the same, but with his musician colleagues. Clearly each person is professionally sensitive in relation to his deepest calling. I conclude from this that I am first and foremost a technician.

Whit Monday. I am spending Whitsuntide in Nancy, with my parents. The last fortnight's tiredness and failures have utterly cast me down. I very much appreciate my parents' reaction to my efforts. My mother is more of an optimist, my father more difficult. There has never been any family smugness with us. I would like to give them a better bill of health. I talk very little about concrete music, while they are eager for details. Basically, they say, we should have made you into a composer! And this remark fits in with earlier reflections.

May 15. Two possible solutions: use the plot as it has come down to us, or else give a new version. Hospital. Eurydice is in a coma. Orpheus is at her side. He brings her back through a sort of tension of the will that could snatch her from death. But there is that look that kills and that he gives to the dying woman, whereas, left to herself, she would have followed him willingly . . . Pooh . . . what a bore!

The real subject of *Orphée* is metaphysical. It's on the theme of the forbidden fruit, much more on the reason for the "why" of the interdiction than the "why" of the fault. At least, only the first interests me. The second is commonplace. It's moral, and it's a story. Orpheus weeps for the lost Eurydice, but as soon as she is found he loses her because he's no longer weeping for her. The metaphysical plot involves the fateful chance event or the malice of the gods. Cocteau makes Eurydice stumble, and Orpheus is taken unawares by his crime.

May 16. The smallest of my worries, in this *Orphée*, is the plot. In this at least I am well within tradition: if the opera is good, the libretto doesn't matter! Nevertheless, I am beginning to have sufficient material, "orchestral pieces." I shall have to think about the lyrical plot of the work, since lyricism there is. My Orpheus sings; he needs a text. My characters are in search of a scenario. Making them one will be the least of my worries. The problem is elsewhere.

May 16. Basically, I'm telling a lie. The theme of *Orphée* is of utter importance to me. All I think about is neglecting the music and spending all my time on the scenario. The recent experience of the *Consul* would incline me all the more, if there were any need, to think of opera as one of the forms of "total spectacle" that I have always dreamed of.

But there we are: my lyrics, my duets, are very much determined by my concrete orchestra. So I am going to keep to the Mickey Mouse scenario, the puppet characters very much in the style of a fairground show, which I thought best to adopt. Already a failure musically, inconsistent in substance, this *Orphée* is coming into being like a monster, is constructing itself like the cells of a cancer. So I will fail courageously. But what I can expect meanwhile is, for sixty hours a week, a veritable time in Hell.

12

End of the second journal. Heautontimoroumenos. *The conductor of potentiometers. A space dialectic. Trio with oneself. Five good minutes. They ask too little of us.*

The second journal ends on May 16, the date on which a vague scenario was sketched out. The more honest situation, which was to put concrete music to the service of a new kind of lyrical work, was unfortunately impracticable. How can we launch ourselves into a three-act opera when we don't know if the singers can be accompanied by the concrete orchestra? And how can we give a year of research to a concrete opera when we can't tell whether it will be effective or not? Will it be only just bearable for the audience, and for quite a long time? And so we could only do a trial run, an exploration taken just far enough. It was of no importance whether the plot was purely conventional, just a dramatic pretext, provided that the lyrical climate allowed us to test the mettle of several pieces from the public and the stage points of view: two or three melodies for Orpheus, a duet with Eurydice, a trio with two or three other characters, one or two passages of choreography or mime. However, we had to maintain a certain coherence that would allow it to be staged. The experiment would be attempted only in front of an invited audience, very small, but it was important that it should be under the usual public performance conditions. We had six weeks until July 20, the date booked for our "performance" at the *Empire*.

I sorted through the materials we had accumulated. I kept the best, so, by force of circumstances, adopting a back-to-front method: these materials led or did not lead to orchestral fragments, which were or were not suited to singing. The nature of these pieces gradually determined the characters, with the result that a very simplified action constructed itself, without my being able to intervene except as coordinator. Embroiled in such a crazy adventure, I wondered if I was my own worst enemy . . . But it didn't matter: I wasn't seeking success, but only to create the conditions for an experiment, which should answer the questions raised by our concert at the Ecole Normale de Musique. The experiment that we were going to attempt at the *Empire* would include some visual elements that had been absent from the concert. If we managed to transform the listener into a spectator, the future would open up to us. If not, we would be demonstrating that concrete music should stay in the laboratory, and we must resign ourselves to looking upon it merely as an accessory.

The test at the *Empire* would be taken in two stages: a second performance of the *Symphonie pour un homme seul*, revised and corrected since the Ecole Normale de Musique; and *Orphée*, which meanwhile had changed its name and was called *Toute la lyre* (The whole lyre).

The main concert hall at the *Empire*, far too huge for an audience of a few hundred, was, however, a good place for experiments because of the acoustics. Once the lights went down, the projectors focused on Maurice Le Roux, framed in the shining bars of the "potentiometric three-dimensional portico," a masterpiece that we owed to the patience and ingenuity of my colleagues but which nevertheless was still only an imperfect step on the way. In his right hand Maurice Le Roux held a ring with four ropes tied to it; his left hand controlled the overall dynamics. In charge of the three-dimensionality and of some margin of nuance, the musician at the desk gave the classical Radio "mixers" a long-awaited revenge: he expanded the nuances instead of compressing them. As for the stereophonic equipment, we were not trying to restore a preexisting depth, as in ordinary stereophonics, but to provide the sound objects of concrete music with a spatial development in keeping with their forms.

I myself had had to experiment for too long on the three-dimensional projection to know precisely at what point an uninformed audience would be able to perceive the phenomenon. So I eagerly scrutinized their reactions, and to my great surprise I saw that, even if they were unskilled in discerning the elements of the phenomenon before them, they were nevertheless touched by it. They felt that something was going on that they remained unable to define. Nonetheless, the *Symphonie* passed in an atmosphere of meditative silence that we had never before obtained. André Moles, on whom more later, who had come from Marseilles especially to be at the performance, immediately sent me a letter in which he said:

> The term "stereophonics" does not seem right for what you are attempting here. This word suggests a re-creation of three-dimensionality, i.e., of the form of the sound source—an orchestra or a dialogue, for example—based on the *criterion of truth*, i.e., trying to re-create the impression a member of the audience would have, shutting his eyes in the concert hall.
>
> The experiments you are doing are much more interesting: leaving aside the criterion of truth, they are aiming at a *new effect* of such importance that I feel it is no overstatement to speak of a new form of musical art. In the same way that music is a dialectic of duration and intensity, the new procedure is a dialectic of sound in space, and I think that the term *spatial music* would be more appropriate than stereophonics.

After the *Symphonie*, the curtain eventually rose on *Orphée*. And it immediately fell again, as a result of a technical hitch on the three-dimensional console. A quarter of an hour later, Maria Ferès, standing alone on the set, was about to sing for the first time without the help of an orchestra, and she accompanied with her touching presence and her extraordinary voice a music that was pretty inhuman, at least in its novelty.

The *Symphonie* had been a surprise. *Orphée*, which was expected to be a new opera, seemed to lack boldness. In fact, despite the concrete music, it all went just the same as at the opera. As for the libretto, I knew better than anyone how bad it was, truly worthy of tradition.

Three quarters of an hour later, Orpheus was alone at front of stage after Eurydice had fled, returned to the shades. This time the text reached a less astonished audience:

They say
That headless
Orpheus
Still called her
Called still
Eurydice
Eurydice
And in echo
Dark Hebrus
Beseeches
Beseeches
Eurydice
Eurydice

Orpheus bent down, picked up a mask—a replica of his own face— held it at arm's length, and began to sing a duet with himself. Then, picking up a second mask with his other hand, he finished with a trio of undeniable pathos. This final melody, over which I had taken much care, was accompanied by a rather extraordinary concrete orchestra, in which gong sounds manipulated by the *phonogène* and the much sought-after "intake of breath" accompanied the rending of the red veil that at the beginning of the last act Maria Ferès held before her with outstretched arms and which she really tore, spasmodically. Perhaps these last five minutes justified the whole work?

What lesson could we learn from all that? Give up concrete music for opera, or opera for concrete music? There were backers for both so- lutions. Some people found us too far removed from traditional music; others, on the contrary, like Messiaen and Henry Michaux, advised absolute originality and breaking off all connections with traditional music.

And so we were urged to move away not only from music, but even from all language: Messiaen was shocked by the continuity of the hu- man voice accompanied by concrete music. Michaux said that lettrism had its points. Lévi-Strauss remarked that the voice can have uses other than singing. After the universe of music, we had to abandon the universe of text, renounce the modulations of the human voice, turn our backs on the explicit. We were being beckoned toward incantations that had no reference to anything.

13

Trouble in Switzerland. Germanic approval. International mistrust. You often need someone more abstract than yourself. In which a concrete physicist appears. A heuristic definition. Cybernetic viewpoints.

Finally, after four years, an insulting letter! It took a bit of waiting for! And it's from Switzerland. For, the world being topsy-turvy, we're prophets in our own country.

> Come on, Gentlemen of Geneva, you must be able to do better than this; you might as well go on holiday! Give this inventor-engineer from Paris an extra allowance and let him have his third experiment in sound effects for free.
>
> Poor us, having to listen to such mediocrity; and this is nothing, for—we've been told—there's a new session next week. Come on, Programmers, have you still got your heads on your shoulders, or have you really been so warped professionally? —J. B.

It's been sent on to me by Robert Ferrazino, a pioneer in concrete music in Switzerland. But, to be fair, I must point out that the same mail contained a letter from a supporter. He demands a full-length concert and asks if there are any records on the market. The Swiss Broadcasting Company, of course, agrees with the grouch and changes the time of the broadcast. In short, a normal country! In the *Tribune de Genève* (July 27, 1951), the worthy William Rime soothes with one hand, threatens with the other:

> Worthy of interest though they are, the experiments in concrete music nevertheless have no affinity with any sort of music, be it polyphonic, atonal, or dodecaphonic, and we cannot prevail enough upon this clever sound technician to modify his terminology if he wants to avoid musicians, concerned to defend their art, declaring a real offensive.

Thanks to Switzerland, the problem was stated in no uncertain terms, and the scandal, certainly not hoped-for but expected as inevitable, could well break out even after such a long time. However, at the same time a paper was given at Darmstadt at the Internationale Ferienkurs für neue Musik (International Summer School for New Music). The *Symphonie* was welcomed enthusiastically there, and one after the other Radio-Cologne, Hamburg, Munich, Baden-Baden broadcast long extracts. Who was right? The Swiss who rejected it and refused to call it "music," or the Germans who anschlussed it somewhat rapidly under the banner of *elektronische Musik* (electronic music)? The titles of the talks in Darmstadt were significant: "Die Klangwelt der elektronischen Musik" (The sound world of electronic music). I found I had quite a few ideas in common with my German colleagues (or, rather, a similar desire to know), but I didn't believe in their *elektronische Musik*, which to my mind was entirely focused on means of execution that had little chance of changing musical ideas. To my great surprise, and all credit to the German technicians, I saw them give ground quite willingly, immediately adopting positions that I no longer even had to defend. Some time later, Radio Munich gave an hour and a half's airtime to an explanation of concrete music that I intend to take as a model.[1]

---

1. In particular, a comparison of the picture and sound montages of M. Günther Bialas, of the Detmold College of Music:

> Today no one would deny the boundless artistic potential of the cinema. Well, just as film, before it came into its own, was no more than filmed theater, so electronic music initially limited itself to reproducing existing sound forms, and it is only now, thanks to the research of P. Schaeffer, Pierre Henry, and Dr. Meyer-Eppler, that it has created an entirely new musical material.

At the Aix-en-Provence Festival some days later, the regional committee of UNESCO organized a debate. Concrete music was in the hot seat, along with dodecaphonic music.

This time I had to defend it across green baize, under the benevolent but very cautious chairmanship of Roland-Manuel. Despite myself, stances hardened. Aix was echoing Geneva. After having argued with me over the concept of the sound object, which is indeed unusual, and listened with interest both to my explanations and several records (played too rapidly and under very bad technical conditions), the learned assembly was divided on the question of whether this was music or not.

Let us pass over the dispute about terminology. Beyond the question of terminology I am happy to enter into debate: in the same way, where figurative and nonfigurative painting are concerned, the debate, if it is about the word painting, is of no interest. It should be about the thing itself. In other words, painting fifty years ago was a representation, and also, it goes without saying, an interpretation. The cubist break with this introduced a new subject for painting, so-called abstract painting. Similarly, with Western music, for centuries music was expression, i.e., language. Suddenly concrete music to some extent breaks with this, and instead of language it introduces an object that no longer has to express itself. The contrasting adjectives— "abstract" for painting and "concrete" for music—in fact demonstrate how alike they are. Classically, music and painting are indeed at opposite poles from each other, at the two poles of reality. Painting is born of an external reality, a spatial and material world. Music, which can be nonfigurative, is born of an inner reality. It is easy to establish connections between concrete music and abstract painting, tangible realities, whereas descriptive music is as illusory as musical painting. Some works of concrete music immediately call for graphic translation, and it would not be impossible, for example, to compose a concrete music based on an abstract painting and which would express the similarities of matter and form. Such a painting would in any case be a better score than notes on lined paper. And so there are indubitably connections between these two new phenomena that build a bridge, this time firm, between painting and music.

Often, in the course of the doubts that assailed me over these last four years, I would take heart by thinking that the adventure begun by cubism was continuing under my very eyes. And yet painters had been faced with the problem of a new art for fifty years without its being so clearly resolved. How, after four years, could we reasonably demand of concrete music that it define itself as a new music or as an antimusic? Perhaps we should have baptized it "plastic music" or "sound plastic"? Why would I, who often left the studio as sick at heart as from an exhibition of modern painting, tempted to destroy it all, have persevered if not because of that great precedent? Several generations of painters had persevered in abstract painting, which some of them were even beginning to call "concrete," in just the same way that I could have called what we had undertaken "abstract music." Only the future would give answers, and perhaps there would be several.

In any case, apart from aesthetic problems, an already considerable experience of the sound world and its physical components, its psychic resonances, convinced me of our contemporaries' lack of competence in this matter. Without in any way being a fan of mechanical progress, I was forced to think that the world of sounds could not indefinitely be strings, piano, ondes Martenot. I could no longer ignore the extraordinary refinement of the ear that my colleagues and I had acquired over the last four years. Perhaps concrete music was not music? Perhaps it never would be? A huge field of experimentation lay open. It needed to find adherents in the very near future, not only musicians, painters, and artists in general but also physicists, psychologists, and serious researchers in the field of aesthetics.

The number of researchers working in this area at the moment is small compared with other sciences. Acoustics, it must be clearly recognized, lags very far behind. After the period of Helmholtz there was a time of disillusionment that lasted until twenty years ago. The laboratories are badly equipped. The people who have rethought acoustics are for the most part Anglo-Saxon. But what about double specialization, where an acoustician considers music for its own sake, and a musician has an objective understanding of acoustics? A double specialization that gives a way into the *no-man's-land* that separates art and technology.

There is, to my knowledge, only one such specialist in France: André Moles, head of research at the C.N.R.S., whose chosen subject for his thesis is precisely *La structure physique du signal en musique microphonique*

(The physical structure of the signal in microphonic music). I've had the manuscript of this thesis before me for just a few days. I must say what satisfaction this well-written and in every respect scrupulous piece of work gives me. Moreover, in the introduction I can see everything that I have come to think from the very first months of my own research. Moles's stance tallies so precisely with mine that with his permission I shall quote at some length from his introduction:

> Music is the most ancient of the temporal arts. The others—dance, cinema, animated drawing—have some contact with spatial arts and, in the aesthetic sensation they arouse, it is often difficult to determine just how much they have to do with temporal perception.
>
> Like time itself, its medium and matter, music is fleeting, passes, and until very recently has never had the concrete nature of sculpture, painting, or architecture, where the material medium survives over time. Music did not exist without performance, and as the score had only a very distant relationship with the musical work, it was not possible to judge the latter independently of performance. And perhaps it is also its fleeting nature that has given music one of its major procedures, *repetition*, without which no other music would exist except the harmonies of the external world, a poor medium indeed for musical creation. Whereas all other art forms have depended on the value *resemblance*, until very recently nothing similar has guided the musician in his creation: this is the unique, almost abstract, characteristic of music, which has made it the most obscure of all the arts, and on which a large body of literature has been written without much benefit to the musician.
>
> Many attempts have been made to define an aesthetics of music, but every one so far seems to have failed; it has been impossible to define a rational overall structure for music because of that very fleetingness that made it elude all objective assessment. Aestheticians in the last century, among whom Charles Lalo is the most famous, were able only to note the extraordinary complexity of the musical motif. Written out in the form of a score, it is a masterpiece of precision and shows how far removed from approximation music seems to be. And this is in contrast with the apparent arbitrariness of the rules of musical composition where progress seems to be made only by methodically breaking the rules previously established . . .
>
> Looking for definitions is useful only insofar as it enables the facts to be grasped. It is interesting that most definitions of music are largely inade-

quate: creating a rhythm, articulating inner time, cutting up time, etc. . . . all these expressions can be summed up in the very general term: music is a *modulation of duration.* As the value of a definition should be heuristic, we will stay with this one, linking it to the concept of *information.*

Music is made to be heard: without listening it would not exist, and its physical and psychological aspects have remained for a long time difficult to discern. In reality, there is very little to add to what Helmholtz said on this subject in his remarkable introduction to the *Leçons sur la physiologie théorique de la musique* (Lessons on the physiological theory of music): for a very long time musical acoustics has been only a part of acoustics concerned specifically with the making of instruments, and an area of psychology concerned with rhythmic sound impressions. It emerged as a discipline in its own right at the time when the movement and development of techniques of amplification, recording, and transmission gave music a material medium with the same relationship to it as the book to literature.

In reality recording techniques apply time to space. Consequently time takes on the properties of space:

- *permanence.* the musical work is defined by its recording, together with all the characteristics added to the score by the conductor.

- *reproducibility,* which makes what could previously only be a comparison between points of view into an object of science.

- *reversibility.* a recording tape can just as well be played backward as forward. Yet time is irreversible—that is its essential nature—and measuring it is always approximate, as it is impossible to establish the equality and the sum of two nonjuxtaposed parts since they cannot be laid end to end. This is not true of space, and only by applying space to time can we measure the latter objectively (using clocks or recording devices).

The usual scientific methods can then be applied to music, the most important being the method of concomitant variations, and objective perceptual factors that are otherwise difficult to quantify can be obtained from the musical signal.

We therefore believe that we can answer the question: "Can the musical signal be defined, described, measured?" in the affirmative. A priori one might wonder if such a study would be of any interest other than speculative . . .

M. Moles's work goes a long way toward answering the thorny questions that my colleagues and I were struggling with. At the very beginning

of A. Moles's thesis I found a diagram that anticipated the procedure
that I had used to define the "complex note," a sound element with three
dimensions: frequency, duration, and dynamic. André Moles has gone
to the extent of calculating the precise number of these sounds, which
make up, in effect, the atomic structure of music, and he has counted
them, as if following the physicists of his day, who go so far as to count
the number of electrons in the universe. He has come up with a number.[2] These sound atoms are indeed the building blocks of all noise, every
sound, all music through the variety of their combinations. Here, those
who make a distinction between a musical and any other kind of experiment will have great difficulty in finding a dividing line. Everything
that the ear registers is made up, to a greater or lesser extent by chance, to
a greater or lesser extent deliberately, of a fair number of musical atoms
obeying an internal mechanism of greater or lesser complexity. The coherence of this way of seeing things leads us away from crude *phonogènes* to
electronic instruments, not in the sense of sound-wave devices—like
Martenot's or Trautwein's—but machines of cybernetics. In effect, only
machines like this (probably weighing several tons and costing hundreds
of millions!) with a certain amount of memory provided by oscillating
circuits, will make possible the infinite variety of complex numerical combinations that are the key to all musical phenomena. We are beginning
to devise and build reading machines, i.e., devices to translate graphic
representations into sounds. These are the first machines that truly speak.
Similarly, there could be machines able to transpose the world of space
into a world of duration. Going back to the previous example, these machines would be capable of transposing a pictorial composition into
sounds. Minds that are enclosed in some false philosophical spiritual-
ism will balk at this thought, and the word "robot" will be pronounced
(in a somewhat robotlike way). We are not expecting an automatic symphony from such machines, but limitless resources for the willed creation
of a symphony. Everything will depend on the picture to be read, and
the functional relationships that the artist-technician establishes between

2. Thirteen million *pure* notes, but a very much greater finite number of perceptible
sounds, having determined values of frequency, timbre, and duration.

space and time values. We are not very well placed. In fact, at the moment we are subject to human automatic behaviors, psychic or mechanical, those that continually haunt our minds or condition the composer's or the violinist's nerves and muscles. In relation to music, we behave very much like talking machines: we transpose muscular contractions into sounds, and these contractions are themselves determined by a hidden programming. A sort of "abstract picture" deep within our psyche—this is the plan for all the music we produce.

In music, the problem of progress is the same as everywhere else. It's a question of knowing whether the evolution of man as a creature will keep pace with the progress of his means, and who, *homo sapiens* or *homo faber*, will have the last word?

PART III The Concrete Experiment
in Music

1952

14 The Concrete Approach

You know how much I admire *Petruchka*, but the *Rite of Spring* worries me. It seems to me that Stravinsky is trying to make music out of something that isn't music, in the same way that the Germans apparently (during the Great War) made steaks with sawdust. In any case the native drum is not yet music . . .

So said Debussy.

To judge by his behavior, it is impossible to say whether the composer no longer knows how to compose, or what to compose, or why to compose. The creative act has lost its necessity. So he invents it. He sets up a working hypothesis, and his whole production between the wars is a huge aspiration toward music, a desperate searching for lost time, by way of the "inauthentic." The musician gives himself not so much a work to make as a new way of making, a new technique, a new type of object; hence that rapid succession of strange, if not mad, forms that have so disconcerted audiences and that are no longer aesthetic projects but fads.

These are the words of Ernest Ansermet, in a most fascinating lecture that he gave in Geneva in 1948, and from which we shall quote at length.

"When the motive for it has vanished," Ansermet goes on, "art can only give a degree of solidity to its projects through dogmatism and formalism. This is true of most aesthetics today, and also true of the two most striking creative innovations of this time, Schönberg's and Stravinsky's."

Probably Ernest Ansermet has never heard of concrete music. So it is all the more interesting to find in such a lucid analysis several points that coincide with our own conclusions. That concrete music presents itself as a "new way of making," is concerned with "a new type of object," is all too clear. At least it is to our credit that we do not claim to produce a work of art straightaway, that our works are constructed in the name of techno-aesthetic experimentation only and not as a true "project." If these procedures have often appeared to us ourselves as both desperate and often inauthentic, then it's because, filled with a taste for the old music, we felt very uncomfortable with this endless groping in the dark. Finally, if audiences have not rejected our efforts, I give thanks neither to heaven, nor to the audiences, nor to us. Rather, as Ansermet predicts, I see in this such uncertainty, such a determination to accept anyone or anything—in short, such a lack of seriousness—that I don't really trust it. If that is the case, concrete music will be a short-lived fad; it will please and displease, it will surprise and just as quickly weary. For the moment, the concrete experiment in music has nothing to do with the audience's tastes or the whims of fashion. On the contrary, it may be that it has to ally itself, much more than we thought at the beginning, with the two experiments that Ansermet sums up so clearly as "the two most striking creative innovations of our time." Concrete music flourishes between two poles, and it could sway them a little. It could be said that it is not without points in common with the two opposed worlds of Stravinsky and Schönberg. Far from reconciling them, however, it could put them into even greater opposition by shedding light on what they bring that is new, and what still chains them to the past.

Without in any way intending to set myself up as the leader of a school or a musicologist, and in any case not having any claim to such pretensions, I have endeavored to write these notes in the same spirit as the new musical development I had happened to discover. I have no theory to put forward, no new musical system. I feel as if I have, almost as a trespasser, entered new attics in this ancient dwelling. I do not know, and doubtless I will not know for some time yet, if these attics are inhabitable, whether they are a temporary prison cell or will be apartments of the future. At least I have tried to enable my reader to follow me, not through dogmatism shored up with endless arguments, but in a practical way, clarified by anecdotes. I could have stopped at this second journal, but I thought I should note down some personal reflections, the fruit of long periods of meditation, thinking that I would not fully have completed my task—I was going to say "my imposition"—if I did not spare others the very great waste of time, the confusions and the misunderstandings inherent in the complexity of the problem of music as it is presented to our contemporaries.

In truth, if there is to be a "concrete" school, it goes without saying that the word "concrete" will only do as a temporary banner, or rather a partial label. The "concrete" aspect of concrete music is clear enough for us to be able to insist on the processes of abstraction that it requires. If, on the contrary, concrete music had only aimed at "concretizing" music, thereby continuing the historical development where instrument makers and composers, makers of clavichords, viols, ondes, and trautoniums, tried to outdo each other in ingenuity, there would merely have been new instruments, building with greater or lesser success on conventional patterns. German electronic music illustrates this quite well.

In reality, concrete music, no sooner than it has been discovered, has been overwhelmed, not only by the proliferation of material but also by the explosion of forms. Far from emphasizing its creative powers in the material sense (as is generally done by the "makers" of new instruments), it turns away, as if wearied by this excess of riches, and clamors for a little bit of order, a cataloging of the objects that have been almost inopportunely set free, an emergency ordering to allow them to be used—in short, some directions for use, even if they are only entirely provisional working hypotheses.

So concrete music cannot be relied upon to provide an immediate solution to the problems raised by contemporary music, any more than
concrete music finds immediate answers in the tradition of Stravinsky
or Schönberg. Nor can we compare the problems of the musicians who
came before us and our own, or say they have nothing in common, or
that they are alike in every respect. It seems to me that they have similarities as do two types of geometry that differ by an extra dimension,
just as some geometrical dead ends are suddenly opened up by a new
geometry, while the new geometry, even if it rejects the propositions of
the old one, nevertheless rests solidly on known ground. Thus, generaliz-
ing the concept of melody still involves referring to the concept of melody; and the concept of instruments involves relying on the concept of
the orchestra. Readers will remember the lengthy procedures described
earlier, when sometimes classical musical values still have meaning,
while at other times they no longer do.

If we follow Ernest Ansermet in his analysis—and it is difficult to see
why he should not be followed—all music (but, let it be understood, Western music) can be summed up by the use of the crucial phenomenon, the
dominant. Insofar as the mystery of music resides in the affective correspondence between the number that expresses relationships of frequency
and human sensibility, and insofar as it absolutely clear (perhaps not to
everyone, but this would need a whole lecture) that every scale, tempered
or not, from Zarlino, Pythagoras or Bach, is based, more or less, on the
fifth and the octave, i.e., the simplest relationships, 2/1 and 3/2, it can be
said that all "melody becomes a certain way of following (or not following) this path, a certain *intention* toward the dominant or a complex of
dominants—for the dominant has determined the pitch, and hence it is
implicit in all our melodic footsteps and is present everywhere."

Where Ansermet completely resolves a debate that has remained obscure for most musicians is when he shows that the classical correspondence between the musical object and the subject who experiences it
evokes a feeling of innerness, of authenticity, and so also of radiance in
the depths of human sensibility, ranging from sadness to joy. So it is not
about pleasure, or beauty, or ugliness; rather, it is about a perfect confor-
mity between man, who is sensitive to the dominant, and a music that

exploits the phenomenon of the dominant, even negatively. "For melody there is only one way to become significant, and that is to be experienced as a pathway. A pathway is still a trajectory, but a trajectory that I complete. The event that is the melody is then interiorized, and the *pathway* as an inner event can take many directions."

There could thus be an explicit way of putting music into direct contact with ethics; the key to this art would be the dominant, i.e., a description of the degrees of scales (innumerable scales—all scales perhaps—are part of this phenomenon). Outside the dominant, no salvation. Except if somewhere else, in other phenomena not linked with the degrees of pitch of sounds, a new form of communication is found, a new aspect of the secret correspondence between the cosmos and man, which Sartre calls "the metaphysical content of the perceptible" and which is everywhere, either as intimations or diffusely. It could be, of course, that the public, on the threshold of this gateway, should read its somewhat Dantesque inscription. Not to lose all hope, but at least to abandon the hope of finding pleasures, emotions, sadness, or joy comparable to those of the dominant universe. Perhaps this will be a new asceticism, with thorny, and possibly dizzying, pathways toward other, less comfortable, heavens.

I shall return later to the inevitable confrontation—or what for me became inevitable despite my unwillingness—between concrete music on the one hand and contemporary musical worlds, polarized by Stravinsky and Schönberg. For greater clarity later on we should give a full description of what we mean by the concrete movement in music.

When Wagner uses the brass, much more for the brass sound than for the melody he gives them (or at least melody and matter are indissolubly linked here); when instrument and violin makers do their utmost to define more and more refined sounds; when composers orchestrate musical ensembles with heightened attentiveness and with defter and more delicate art; when, after the already highly significant experiments of Debussy and Ravel, Stravinsky, according to Ansermet, makes the first assault on music "animated from within" and sanctions modern music's entering into the inauthentic, then in reality the need is being clearly expressed to create music, not just in the form of a blueprint, but from within the context of the sounds themselves.

Conversely, if, in each period of time, the development of musical forms is characterized by the use first of various consonances, then of various dissonances (and the frontier between them is fluid and only validates habits of listening); if Debussy discovers and introduces the six-tone scale; and if, then, contemporaries pursue the systematic use of ancient or new modes, notably Messiaen's modes of limited transposition, before arriving at the dodecaphonic system, we are indeed forced to recognize a development by increasing complication, by the gradual introduction of a syntax, which, for all its greater complexity and subtlety, does not any the less use the same words, or at least the same signs representing the same values, i.e., notes.

Now, in its concrete as in its abstract aspect, contemporary music is limited in its development by the very means of "making music" and "writing music down." This is precisely where the concrete movement comes in.

As long as we stay with ordinary instruments and the usual symbolism, the formal and material development of music will necessarily be limited to combinations of instruments and combinations of notes. On the one hand, the tendency of the Stravinskyists will be to lay the emphasis on discoveries of matter (and there certainly are plenty to be found within an ordinary orchestra), and the Schönbergians' tendency will be to develop more and more abstract structures (where combinations of notes in new relationships will be the most important thing of all in this trend, which bears no relationship with orthodox musical experience).

It would be a mistake to try and see two entirely separate trends in Stravinsky and Schönberg, one leading toward the concrete, the other toward the abstract in music. We must immediately balance what we have just put forward by presenting the other side of the argument.

Stravinsky's world is indeed focused on the abstract, whereas, like it or not, Schönberg's poses, or at least supposes, a concrete context. Insofar as Stravinsky seeks to escape from one sound dimension, pitch, he uses a distinctive meter, dissociated, as it were, from the melodic articulation. In short, he is not so far from rhythmic series, where bar, not note, succeeds bar, each of these bars having a different structure, with no repetition. Schönberg, for his part, in his treatise on harmony, wishes for a *Klangfarbenmelodie* of the future, which would consist of creating a melody of timbres on, for example, a sound of a given pitch. An abstract preoccupation with Stravinsky, a concrete one with Schönberg, we can immediately recognize two notions on which concrete music can definitively shed light: the idea of creating new and relatively autonomous dimensions of musical expression by using parameters of sound other than pitch. Stravinsky does not have the means of creating cells in the concrete music sense, but his classic bars, although they are composed of rational notes and rhythms, are very close to this. Schönberg, in the *Klangfarbenmelodie*, sees only a succession of sounds taken from a variety of instruments on one position in the tessitura (which could be very thin and might be confused with a unison), but both are nevertheless important initiatives, which new and original means may allow to develop fully.

Despite the interest and importance of these precursors, it is nevertheless true that Stravinsky's "polymetry" and Schönberg's *Klangfarbenmelodie* appear in their works only as minor phenomena or as experiments with no meaningful development. On the other hand, these two musicians are at the top of the bill for discovery, with two major stances summed up in the words "polytonality" and "atonality."

And so finally ends a musical development that certain signs showed to be going nowhere. It is, of course, presumptuous to think that there will be no other Ravel, no other Bartók, that there is no longer anything to say, anything to discover, in a sound world where the most savage detractors of the dominant nonetheless use "material" where the dominant has been present for centuries; but, like it or not, what the most ingenious and the boldest musicians will never be able to obtain is that what has been has not been, i.e., that ears stop hearing the notes of the scale, whether of six or twelve tones, from outside their listening habits, in other words, as if suddenly cut off from a musical civilization that has put its mark so strongly on the West.

Let us make no mistake. When for the first time we use the third, or the second, or the seventh or the dominant, we are not creating a totally new music. We are playing an ancient music with this new element incorporated into it, not only for its specific contribution, but also for the break it makes with ancient customs. By continuous accretions like this, the listener evolves into the composer; in every age, the generations take in a new word, a new figure in a rhetoric that remains recognizable, and therefore comprehensible, through continuity. When Debussy gives a six-tone scale, is it a six-tone scale that we hear? Certainly not; we hear it only in relation to the old cadences, an underlying leading note, and not at all as a newborn baby brought up exclusively with Debussyism would hear it, or as a native South African suddenly initiated into this sound universe would. Newborn baby and primitive man would hear Debussy's scale with a quite different ear from Debussy himself. The same goes for the dodecaphonists. One of their mistakes, among others, is to think that they can construct an atonal series. Those who hear them, and doubtless they themselves, will recognize (and perhaps secretly use) the forbidden fruit, the remains of former savors. And so the most authentic of them are motivated by an incredible will for destruction, using an orthodox musical material, and at the same time disfiguring it: this is the painful contradiction for anyone who, without any inventive genius of his own, wants to follow Schönberg's literal legacy. It's either one thing or the other: either such works are listened to with a tonal "subtext," fragmentary and as it were clandestine, or else the series is so rigorously used that it is no longer a question of hearing music in the sense retained, through continuity, of this word: it is simply sound objects put together in combinations of twelve sounds, where the note plays the same part as the letter for lettrists. A good lettrist poem should of course be rigorously dissociated from all echoes, a word or an onomatopoeia. At the moment serial music is in the same boat as concrete music. It is breaking away from musical language; it is not even music, except that it is played with instruments and musical signs, whereas, at the outset, concrete music was made with noises and plastic signs.

We shall come back in chapter 17 to this essential question of musical language. For the time being, let us get this point clear: whether we're dealing with extending sounds, using a wider and wider register of timbres, in which timbre itself has expressive value through its development, or whether we're dealing with combining sounds where every effort is made to consider sounds of a given pitch as merely pawns in a game, stones of a building, it can be seen that, willingly or not, there is a moving away from traditional musical material. Willingly, in the case of Stravinsky, who, in theory, would be thought (though perhaps wrongly) to approve of concrete music. Not, in the case of the dodecaphonists, who were very hostile to the beginnings of concrete music, which in fact held a strange power of attraction for them. The only true atonality, ultimately, is in concrete music if the elements of a series do not trigger any association of ideas based on tonality. But there is nothing against making a tonal concrete music, which my colleagues, let us say (I daren't say "disciples"), with dodecaphonist sympathies would like to proscribe. In buildings where everything is new and surprising, the decision not to have a single familiar element seems to me arbitrary, and, what is more, inhuman. I see a hint of snobbery, or, more precisely, a very modern prejudice, a bias toward the unheard that I do not share. That in my own efforts to construct concrete works in which the dominant would still dominate, but in a new way, I have failed, I admit, but that is not the last word. I hope and pray for other (let us say) disciples, who, without wishing to put wine that is too new into skins that are too old, would endeavor to reconnect with musical tradition: to develop without rejecting, break away without destroying, contribute something undeniably new to music, yet without making people stop listening to the language that we quite rightly consider to be the language of civilized people.

Polytonality, atonality; should I say that, despite my admiration for Stravinsky and my esteem for Schönberg, I am prepared to follow Ansermet in his forecast of decadence, not to say inauthenticity. Rather I will say that these words, which include the word "tonality," still illustrate its use, through excess or default. That there is something sour, exciting but impure, in Stravinsky's use of clichés turned against themselves, something specious, comfortless, in serial music; this is what many people whisper without daring to say so, or say without good enough arguments.

I find with pleasure, from the pen of Luc-André Marcel (and doubtless he as well has not yet heard of concrete music) in a very recent edition of the *Cahiers du Sud,* where he has written a most lucid article on Schönberg, a paragraph that I would like to borrow in order to give a fairly good isometric projection, I would venture to say, of the "concrete development." This paragraph is precisely, according to him, Schön-berg's temptation, and where he would have failed:

> What could a sound absolute be if not a universe made of all sounds? A surface or a sphere where no silence interferes, where there is no break in the perfect relationship of one note to one note, where all of them are prolonged to infinity, in every dimension, not in succession, but simulta-neously. And what about this scale *limitless* in pitch and depth? Isn't it a circle? One single note? Or perhaps even silence? And what is our music if not the very fragile reflection of this immense scale summed up in a sound that is still inaudible to us, a series of more or less accidental and arbitrary breaks that form various scales? If I introduce one single silence into this scale *that contains every sound*, it's done for, division takes place. I perceive differences. Unity is broken. The notion of variety appears and it is possible for notes to follow each other. Music could thus be defined as an art of arranging silences, getting rid of certain sound spaces to cre-ate others and coordinate them. Now Schönberg, I imagine, was not un-likely to indulge in dreams about this absolute and this whole. But it was clear that to approach it he only had the still very primitive tools of present-day sound physics. In order to be heard, he had to follow the mechanics of instruments and use the tempered scale established by the West. He understood its imperfection and impoverishment as well as anyone. He knew what gulf, in truth, separates an F from an F *sharp*. But if he didn't want to be working at compositions in quarter or eighths of tones, the rules of dodecaphonism had first to be fixed. Others, he perhaps thought, when instruments and ears are more refined, will establish a more subtle scale.

15 The Experimental Method

If I chose to quote M. Luc-André Marcel, it is because his expectation of
a new music is expressed both in the sense that these events are happening and in a completely opposite sense. If in fact we happen to notice
symptoms of decadence in an art—or even in a civilization—we can at a
pinch imagine circumstances, or even the conditions, for a renewal, but
rarely does the prophecy go so far as to foresee the new subject of the art,
or the style of the civilization expected. In the same way, what the critic
of Schönberg can see very clearly is the flaw in the system, its arbitrary
limitations, and hence its internal contradictions—and also the beginnings of a renewal and the means of breaking the deadlock, precisely
through the rethinking of what is called sound physics. Where he may
not be such a good prophet is when he gives in to the pressure of the
musical civilization with which he is still imbued and hopes for a more

subtle musical scale, more refined instruments and ears. This does not quite go along with what experience has shown us. Not that the scales, the instruments, and the ears in concrete music should not be, in some way, and are not, in fact, more subtle; but not, of course, in the sense that was expected. In the expected sense, we should more accurately have to say crudeness, imperfection. A revolution, a renewal, nearly always comes about against something, or at the very least through and in order to go beyond a certain state of affairs. But what takes place is something very different. The old universe is superseded, but—fortunately or alas— through a new contribution, which completes nothing, which adds to or replaces, or purely and simply imposes another way of being.

What it is important to understand—and this is one of the problems in this extraordinary age, even though we are helped by a whole context of other discoveries, other revolutions in thought, techniques, and politics—is the radical nature of some changes, for which the preceding centuries and historical continuity have not prepared us. What is more, the perfectly natural tendency to consider one's own age as extraordinary is too common for good minds not to mistrust it as a matter of course. For my part, every time the temptation occurs, and particularly in politics, for example, I would be inclined to remind the enthusiasts, or the panic-stricken, of the eternal renewal of things. Things evolve, go through cycles, and then start again. But then things do not repeat themselves, cycles do. So it is important to know where we are in the cycle, if we are right in the middle of it or exactly at the "singular point" of renewal.

If these comments seem too vague or too general, then let us apply them to the development of music. It is not a matter of debate that the *pianoforte* and temperament are at the root of one of these cycles, for example. Behind the *pianoforte* the orchestra emerges, and as a result of temperament a harmony can be established and noted down on a score. And for several centuries our starting point was a particular music that was able to develop for some time after Bach, without a real revolution. The revolutions called Beethoven, Wagner, Debussy, Stravinsky do not mark a real renewal; they explore a planet where there were still terrae incognitae. Great champions can be surrounded by a crowd of followers or even precursors: one individual is not enough to exhaust a formula or a field where he has nevertheless been an innovator for all time and for everyone.

The same goes for the sciences, but with the difference that the scientist is not, like the artist, required to have absolute originality. A scholar can work in extensive fields, applying original thought that he owes to the genius of his predecessors, yet without being accused of plagiarism. This was true of the Bach family, over the happy centuries when—it must be said—artistic competition was much less fierce, and, for most artists and their public, art had much more to do with pleasure than commitment. In short, the contemporary composer finds himself under the same obligation as the physicist or the analyst, who aspires to fame and an entry in the dictionary: he is asked to discover a new function, a new substance. The teaching in the schools is more than ever derisory: musicians are trained like engineers. Now, whereas we expect engineers to apply procedures that are known and duly taught, we implicitly expect every modern composer to discover a music of his own, which is tantamount to saying that we require a discovery from him, and this not in a field of his own, but in the objective universe of musical knowledge.

The parallel with the writer is also not very precise. The writer uses a language that is not always an end in itself. A novelist, a philosopher, a playwright use language for purposes that are not consistent with the matter and form of language. People will be indulgent toward a writer, even if his style is poor, if what he writes about is sensational. The only possible comparison is with the poet. Now, as in music, so much poetry has been written and read over the last few decades that the field is similarly exhausted; poetry is on the brink of expiring, it appears, because poets no longer interest us unless they are inventors.

We may seem to be going off the subject. But in fact, it was necessary fully to understand the situation that the young composer finds himself in, and which, in addition, he has to deal with without being fully aware of it. Young musicians are like mathematicians fresh from college, who, because they no longer have to reinvent the Cartesian coordinates or the conical section, see themselves obliged to write every memo in the form of a communication to the Académie des Sciences. As many of them, with justification, do not have such pretensions, why should we be surprised

by their infatuation for every master who offers them what a true physicist or analyst gives young scientists? Schönberg shows the way (and a
way that has method, not just example, like Stravinsky) and we are ready
to follow him, to consider him the boss, however unrewarding the experiments he asks us to do. In other words, music presents itself to the most
courageous researchers of our day much more as scientific research than
an expressive art. In these conditions, how can we be surprised at the
naïve eagerness of so many of them to line up series, calculate propor-
tions between rhythm and intervals, and, having done that, once the
result (rarely right) has been given to an orchestra, to defend it vigorously,
without even noticing that this result, which cannot be heard on paper,
and to which they immediately attach a sentimental value—the excess
of tenderness that here they retain from their most sentimental elders—
cannot be appreciated except as an experiment, not as an intention?

This is such a strange, paradoxical situation, at the same time so comic
and tragic, that I would not have had the slightest inkling of it had I not
come to know some of them intimately. How could I disabuse them without in so doing attacking what seems to me, even today, so precious: a
new development in musical research? My intention is not to take to task
the dodecaphonic approach in general. There is a precise and detached
critique of it in the *Cahiers du Sud* quoted above. I am all the more disin-
clined to pick a quarrel with it, as it seems to me that in another sense
the dodecaphonic phenomenon is a preparation for the concrete movement, and quite a few problems raised more radically by the latter were
already implicitly raised by dodecaphonic music. I am thinking particularly of the compulsory dropping of current musical language, and also
of the sensibility that went with it: also a different way of behaving with
regard to the sound object, which the dodecaphonists did not even dare
to bring about openly. We shall return to this later. What I would more
willingly take to task, as M. Luc-André Marcel does so excellently, is "the
pretentiousness of the least of M. Leibowitz's students, who, from the
heights of their alphabet book, pour scorn on the shortcomings of Ravel,
Stravinsky, Bartók, Falla, and Schönberg himself . . . whereas, for Schönberg, principles are only the means for transformation and research, and
are only justified as such. If I determine a certain rule for myself, what

will be the outcome? It was followed by experiment. It is only later that these questionings will be changed into categorical imperatives; for disciples demand miracles at set times." So, I deplore the fact that René Leibowitz, instead of presenting his works as would a modern mathematician, concerned with formulas only insofar as they satisfy physicists and help them either to interpret or to bring about a certain phenomenon, presents them as a conventional musicologist, who limits himself to musical analysis without bothering about the outcome, and who applies principles—and with what a wealth of detail—without even for one moment asking himself how well founded they are in theory or how valid in practice. As long as René Leibowitz treats twelve-tone music like a bible, he will bolt the doors of a dungeon on himself and his colleagues. He is not building on any past in this way, nor is he prefiguring the future.

If the dodecaphonic approach had remained, or if it could go back to being, experimental, it would be quite a different story. If, even from within twelve-sound music, scores were constructed "to find out" in the sense of physicists' "experiments to find out," if these were sanctioned by humble—and not imperious—listening, twelve-sound music could develop and to a certain extent succeed. It would still be necessary for composers, instead of insisting that their diagrams be aesthetic and their series right, to be prepared to get it wrong, and to choose from their diagrams the ones that despite—and, above all, because of—breaking the rules, would awaken some reaction deep within the instinctive musical sensibility.

If the first clash between concrete music and dodecaphonic music has been severe, it is because of this way of going about things. There are already two opposing schools in concrete music. One is for empiricism in construction, which essentially relies on the instinctive ear. The other school, which takes its method from the serial musicians, applies arbitrarily preconceived schemas to concrete matter and relies on the automatic process that then leads from the diagram to the result. Dare I say that the second way of doing things, even if I find it shocking, seems to me more justified in concrete music than in piano or orchestral music? In effect, as there is still nothing to guide us, or to attach us to the past, and thousands of concrete sounds have no reference to usual sounds, objects made "in series" at least do not run the risk of being caricatures of some previous music, or musics that go against nature. We simply have to submit the result of these structures to analysis and above all to the judgment of the ear. Having said this, the fact remains that the paths opened up by the already well-established habits of the dodecaphonists are very specious. They are obsessed by the twelve sounds. And by the precision of the keyboard. To go from twelve to several thousand, and from the tempered keyboard to *phonogènes,* which are still scarcely so, they would have to forget that false rigor, which is old hat, and adopt another method that often horrifies them by its imprecision. It is the same method used by mathematicians and physicists, who are not afraid of approximation—quite the opposite—and for whom this is, through instinct as well as training, the only possible way of approaching real phenomena.

In this way we would be more likely to rediscover Stravinskyan structures, studies in the form of iambs or groupings in pairs, two or three judiciously chosen sounds, varied not according to a linear parameter but by the ear's choice, in keeping with an instinct that is still obscure, although we can discern its resources. If I have the choice between thousands and thousands of sounds, if I can simultaneously vary their pitch, timbre, rhythmic structure, depth, and thickness, it is less important to line them up, imitating the dodecaphonist series, which is, for us, both too complicated and too simplistic, than to sample them, place them in similar or opposing pairs, being particularly careful about rests and silences, which are intended to facilitate listening to them, and not to confuse an ear that has already lost its way in an unfamiliar experience. If it is true that repetition was a feature of the beginnings of all primitive musics, as pebbles mark out a way, why not opt for, rather than (already!) forbid, any repetition in concrete music, on the pretext that it is proscribed under Schönberg? Proscribed there to suppress tonality, here it would be prescribed to make us rediscover music. As Stravinsky's orchestra sketches out melodies, suggests ensembles that are much more trajectories and designs, structures and colors, than themes, harmonies, counterpoints, why not try, out of instinct, to get back to and go beyond Stravinsky, who did not have such plastic means?

But we are running ahead of ourselves. We are always forced to do this, because we cannot start where things begin. People as well are in too much of a hurry, pouncing on the sound objects of concrete music, as authors or as listeners, demanding to find old habits of thought, expression, and technique. If musicians want to follow us, the important thing is that, from the outset, they let go of any traces of their previous behavior. They must turn over a new leaf and above all not ape scientific procedures where they do not apply. This is the worst trap of all.

When good musicians encounter concrete sounds, and despair of being able to make them fit into any theoretical notation, they often turn to the sound engineer, asking for the aid of his measuring devices. A sound, they say, must be able to be measured precisely, and since you have so many parameters, you must be able to measure it all the more precisely: its pitch, its density, its timbre, its power etc. . . . To which the sound engineer, well accustomed to using his various dials, replies that when, for example, he broadcasts a program, he too thinks much more as a musician than as a technician. If he looks at the needle of the "modulometer," it is to get an idea of the "framework" within which he can place a crescendo. If he then manipulates his potentiometer, he does it with the skill of an instrumentalist who, guided by his ear, adapts the movements of his muscles to the resources of his instrument. Apart from the fact that measuring sounds would result in a table of figures compared to which dodecaphonic series are child's play, such a table would be unusable. If composers expect the engineer's instruments to serve as their ear, the situation would soon be reversed: the engineer would expect musicians to provide experimental tests for the study of musical acoustics, or for the psychology of auditory sensations.

So let the composer beware. A sphinx watches over the gateway to every field of human endeavor, to every particular discipline. Whosoever wishes to make music will make it, willy-nilly, through his ear. Whosoever wishes to experiment with a series of figures or machines will, whether he wants to or not, do physics or experimental psychology. And all this work must not lead to waste.

For my own part, what I have to suggest is neither one nor the other, or rather it is both but makes a clear distinction between their various aspects. The apparatus of concrete music, which in effect has revitalized ways of making music, can be tried out in its own right. Sounds as well can be classified and analyzed in their own right, according to their different material, formal, semantic, or psychological content. Art, if it can possibly be attained, is born at the moment when the aesthetic result is in direct contact with the technical means. All science is good, every technique is good, if it leads to an Art that is concerned with both the subject and the object; art is a relationship between subject and object. The exercising of this relationship is the very stuff of art.

16 The Musical Object

The situation in which the contemporary musician finds himself, if he
agrees to approach Music in its concrete form, is very different from the
deadlock that we have tried to define. He was seeking, it seemed to us,
to create the unheard, to build for himself a style so personal that his
originality could not be questioned—in short, to write as no one before
had ever written. In doing so, he claimed to discover and not to express
in his work. Insofar as, for some contemporary musicians, only the dodecaphonist camp seemed to open up a new channel of expression, we have
seen that, without realizing it, they were experimenting and not expressing. They will doubtless protest, but I am obliged to uphold this statement, and if I hadn't made it clear enough, I would repeat that where, on
the part of both the composer and the listener, there has ceased to be
compatibility of language, or an easy process, either for the creator to

construct an expressive object or for the beneficiary to perceive the expression of that object, there is no longer expression. The former, by applying a priori structures, restricts his choices so much that he is no more than a craftsman in the service of a sort of aesthetic automatism; the latter, by attributing his impressions merely to false relationships from the past or to relationships that cannot be perceived directly by the musical sensibility but only by the analytical intelligence, is no longer a listener but the analyst of a written text or a diagram. So there has ceased to be a musical language. There is no longer even a musical relationship between composer and listener through the intermediary of what I have to call a "musical object."

The concept of musical object is far from classic in music. I have recently found that pronouncing these words gave rise to controversy and misunderstanding among many musicologists. This is for several reasons. It is true that the concept itself is new, and its use is new, inasmuch as music is made into the object of knowledge and not only of art.

The concept of object is not mentioned at all in the theory of music, whether in musicianship, harmony, composition, or criticism. The facture of the work, with the symbolism of notation, the structure of forms, and the effect produced, forms a perfectly enclosed whole, sufficient to itself, a closed universe. The musical relationship occurs between the twelve notes of the scale, a composer, and a listener without there being any need to distinguish the musical object itself. (The role of the performers is sublimated or minimized, depending on opinion.) Now, I am obliged to interrupt the learned doctors—I had to do this, and not without difficulty, at the meeting at Aix-en-Provence chaired by Roland-Manuel—to ask them this question: between the moment when the composer finishes his work and the moment when a listener perceives it, is there, yes or no, a zone that is objective, i.e., independent of the subjects who have composed or who will hear, where the music exists in itself, either as a score or as a performance? We don't need to submit this object to the measurements of physicists any more than we need to demand from classical musical theory a phenomenology of it and its relationship to the two subjects it links together. We only have to allow that there is a gap, a *no-man's-land* where nobody ventures. It is not surprising that until now there has been no real science of music, since the very object of such knowledge has not been clearly perceived.

We have seen that the same was true of language. Semantics is a recent discipline, and the need for it, although undeniable, has long been masked by phonetics.[1] Present musical knowledge is, in reality, only a sort of musical phonetics and the rules of a completely fabricated art. The study of musical structures hasn't even been embarked upon, except for the study of what are quite improperly called "forms" (sonata, symphony, etc.), which are simply customary ways of packaging sound ensembles. If we happen to wonder why the melody quoted in chapter 11, figure 15, readily resolves with a symmetry, we are in fact bringing in *Gestalttheorie*, not the rules of harmony. Only the theory of forms inquires why a given symmetry is deemed to be desirable and preferred by both the classical composer and the listener. This new approach is concerned with the relationship of the sound object to the person who chooses or composes it and the person who recognizes and shows himself to be sensitive to it.

This disregard for the concept of the sound object can ultimately be explained for practical reasons. Until very recent times, the sound object, fleeting and tied to the passage of an irreversible and irrecoverable period of time, presented as a human phenomenon much more than an objective fact. There is, in fact, no object of scientific study that cannot be repeated, discerned from the chaos, isolated, and able to coincide with itself when it is examined. Now time—the medium and facilitator of the phenomenon of music (as we saw in chapter 13)—is beyond the reach of the experimenter. No one portion of time can coincide with another. This is so true that we could only apprehend the sound object in the two ways it presented itself: either as a project, the score, or as a "memory" of the performance. (But the performance, no sooner here than gone, and retained only haphazardly by the memory, is all bound up with the complex psychology of the concert.) Hence there is a twofold uncertainty in the understanding of the phenomenon of music, and in particular a twofold

---

1. Also, semantics does not deal so much with the relationship of the word to the person using it, except in the case of *General Semantics* by A. Korzybski.

limitation, one accepting only "notatable" sounds as material for music, the other accepting only "performable" works—and therefore, in the main, performance itself—as an expression of music.

And this is not all. The concealment of the musical object is also due to the distinction made between sound and noise. For, since there have been men who listen, civilizations have painstakingly divided what they hear into two categories: on the one hand sounds (musical or similar), and on the other noises. It is difficult to imagine, unless there were to be some flagrant proof of its necessity, any suggestions to revise this age-old classification, and the appearance of a musical object that, a priori, would not be called either sound or noise. There are indeed transitional zones between musical sound and noise in nature, and in many early instruments, but this zone is by no means objective. Quite the contrary. It has often been used, being considered particularly expressive, by poets, playwrights, and musicians themselves. It is therefore easy for the informed person to announce that something is only sound or only noise, i.e., only music or only sound effects, particularly as the term "sound effects" has, and without any difficulty, gained acceptance. So where would that leave the musical object?

The new element has two aspects. I hope that this has been clear throughout the pages of this journal. On the one hand, the instruments that we have give us access to an infinity of new sounds, which are neither musical in the classical sense nor noises, i.e., they evoke neither pure music nor drama, but they are indisputable sound-beings, filling the whole space—one might say the whole abyss—between the musically and the dramatically explicit. (So how should we not say "sound object"?) On the other hand, once sound is stripped of its fleeting nature, these same instruments allow us to conserve, to reproduce, to make coincide indefinitely with itself a crystallized music, with all the characteristics of its performance, where project and execution, spirit and matter are integrated. How can we not say that this record or that tape, in their entirety, contain the "musical object" in material form?

This crucial fact has many implications, which, whether our findings are accepted or not, should shake the world of music to its foundations. We shall list some of them.

The consequence of limiting music to notatable, performable sounds, which are called "natural"—wrongly, as they are the result of careful instrument making—is that every musical work is built on *structures*, or archetypes, that until now have seemed to be the only "musicable" ones. It is as if mathematicians had not yet discovered irrational numbers, and in their inability to solve the problem of squaring the circle used only algebraic numbers. The whole of mathematics would have been halted. Functions and theories, systems and solutions, everything would have stalled due to the ability to use only a certain type of number. In the same way that analysts have opened the way to entirely new constructions by the introduction—quite scandalous to their contemporaries—of imaginary numbers (i.e., by using a symbolism even more absurd mathematically than concrete sounds are musically), so the notion of the "complex note" clears the way for a field of music that is huge in a different way from the field of the so-called pure note.

On the other hand, however, classical music had to be performed. Not only were the structures used in composition limited, but so were the means of execution. It would be wrong to think that these were limited mainly because of the state of instrument making or the skill of the performers. Personally, I tend to find them both generally satisfactory. The most treacherous limitations, because they are utterly seductive, arise from the fact that music is performed in ensembles, and therefore to the beating of a muscular rhythm. It would be wrong to deny that this is a providential arrangement, leading to a musical humanism "by construction," but to keep to an arithmetically measured music, conducted with a baton, i.e., having, through a process of construction, all the hallmarks of a simple muscular process, is to disregard the huge effort made by man in every domain to tear himself away from his own scale of being, to escape from anthropomorphism, and reach for superrational constructions that would increasingly represent the universe. We could, then, turn Debussy's comment on the African drum on its head and apply it to the Colonne orchestra, which we could see as a primitive drum in the age of atomic theory. Science accustoms minds to think the unthinkable. It familiarizes them not only with dimensions inaccessible to our senses, but even with the fact that the rhythm of the world, physical time, is not the rhythm of the metronome or the biceps. Perhaps it would be a good thing if music, if it still aims to speak the somewhat mysterious language of the gods, turned its mind to more arduous, and above all more objective, constructions?

This consideration leads, of course, to questions about the goal, or rather the various goals, of music. These questions raise others in their turn, in particular whether the concept of an art with the main virtue of pleasing still holds good, or if we are moving on to an art with the singularly more austere virtue of furthering knowledge, completing the means to scientific development through other, specific and complementary, means. These matters are beyond the scope of the present work. They require another, more general work that links the concrete experiment in music with other experiments, with the spiritual destiny of the age. We will make every effort to produce this work one day. For the time being, let us stay with the concept of the musical object, which we are endeavoring to elucidate, and give some practical examples of how such objects come into being, are recognized, and are experimented upon.

From thousands of others, let us take this one: let us suppose that we are recording a sound obtained by lightly rubbing several piano strings with a finger. This "extracting"—as we say in the language of concrete music—requires a technique of its own, and it can give rise to a great variety of sound objects. Depending on the mode of attack (fleshy part of the finger, fingernail, plectrum, etc.), the speed of rubbing, the pressure on the strings, the muffling of the sound, and, above all, the number of strings that are rubbed, we will obtain a sound that is more or less similar to a musical sound or to noise, more or less timbred, matte, or, most importantly, "thick." So here we are suddenly, far removed from the subtlety desired by M. Luc-André Marcel. It's not a question of caviling over an eighth of a tone but of putting into motion a block of several semitones, which we would call a "thick sound," which presents as the generalization of a sound of fixed pitch, a so-called pure sound.

What can be made with a sound like this? First, a kind of melody. Our

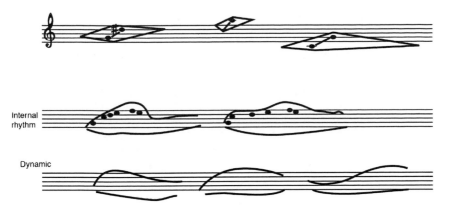

FIGURE 16. [Manipulation of a complex note.]

equipment allows us to "play" this "complex note" in the tessitura (fig. 16), give it rhythm, etc. We can also, without seeking to produce such a banal melodic development, try to create a family of objects similar to the prototype but in which the factor of form would come into play, for example by increasing the intensity or cleanness of attack, by broadening the internal rhythm, or by accentuating the beginning or the end of the sound (fig. 16). This succession of sounds, by transforming the intrinsic form of the object, makes a series, a kind of *antimelody*. It is as if the piano rubbing were considered a little piece of music in its own right, and a suite of variations were created on the formal theme it suggests. Between these two options, then, we come back either to a classical type of development—unless the note played is different from, and richer than, an ordinary note—or to a plastic type of alignment, if it is the case that the plastic consists in arranging objects in relation to each other. Could there not ultimately be a middle term, or more precisely a process that would be neither so classical nor so unexpected, by which I mean neither so musical in formula nor so antimusical in the fact that it implicitly rejects playing a note and consists in lining up a series of objects deemed to have intrinsic relationships with each other, like volumes in a building?

For this to happen there would have to be parameters of musical development other than pitch, in which development in pitch would, at the very least, no longer be the exclusively dominant characteristic. A "series" from the same sound object, identical to itself but affected by different intensities, can in effect constitute a "dynamic melody." There are precedents for this in ordinary music: the repetition of the same note in crescendo, diminuendo, or with sforzandos. In practice, however, we can never be quite sure that the impression of crescendo is exactly the same: the "complex note" can develop more extensive sound impressions than a simple note. A dynamic melody will be able to engage our interest in a way that the same form composed of ordinary notes could not. We would point out another possibility, which is to compose a *Klangfarben-melodie* in the Schönbergian sense: in effect, the thickness of that complex note not only means that its timbre can be acted upon, but also that a correlation can be made between a melody in tessitura and a melody of timbres. Here it would be impossible to understand fully what we are talking about without listening. This experiment, which we are beginning to master (for these final chapters contain certainties that the *Second Journal* did not yet have), shows that such melodies are in this case obtained from a close fusion of the three parameters of musical variation: they are no longer arithmetical and distinct variations of pitch, intensity, and timbre in duration; they are nuanced (and in this case subtle, even refined) developments of all those parameters together. It is doubtless quite difficult to imagine what we are talking about without having come with us to the studio. To make it clearer, we should add that beforehand we will doubtless have transformed the discontinuous and heterogeneous sound of the "complex note" from the "rubbed piano" into a continuous homogeneous sound (this is now possible), which can be sustained like the note of an organ, and which would contain all imaginable attacks as well. The three-dimensional melody that it is now possible to obtain from the original "extract" no longer has anything in common with the initial noise-sound, which is recognizable in varying degrees. If it is well done, it is bright or matte at will, and the ear, surprised at first, quickly becomes accustomed and takes pleasure in sensing the development of matter in that triple space, with its interplay of color and form, permanence and fluctuation. The sound, basically thick, can become thinner, and it can not only evolve in pitch but it can be given a profile there in different ways; at the same time, the "sound color" can be brighter or more matte, and consequently the timbre as well can be varied between high and low. It is at this point that the variations of intensity, i.e., the nuances, go beyond the crude sampling of the earlier experiment. Once it is understood that, while a sound is developing toward the high tessituras, it is now possible to make its timbre lower—and vice versa—we shall understand the new counterpoint that is being opened up for composing complex notes.

In earlier developments, as might be expected, the *phonogène* played a vital part, making it into a new musical instrument that was much more general (but much less convenient at the moment) than conventional instruments. This would seem to bring us back to a music that is also generalized but not completely different from the norm. This is true, but we must immediately recount how, having demolished the sound object made up of the complex note, as it were, and made it into a "homogeneous matter" (which possesses more than qualities, for in doing so we have lost the originality of the attacks, the personal outline of the note, its dynamic profile, etc.), we can, by reversing the process, enrich this object, "blow it up" to the point where it becomes such an important note that we have to call it a "large note." This is what chemists do with certain molecules, which in principle, however, are infinitely simpler and smaller than cells, and which, by means of a kind of inner welding, grow larger and turn into a phenomenon that is materially greater. There are many examples like this in classical music, where clearly much more emphasis is placed on the "sound matter" than on harmonic organization (fig. 17).

The "piano rubbing," it will be remembered, had a certain thickness. We thought that the rubbing, even when made thicker or thinner, would develop symmetrically in the tessitura. What if—while the top of the note remains fixed—we raised or lowered its bottom edge (fig. 18)? What if we moved the two edges either in parallel or in contrary motion? We know that once the note has been attacked, it is in our power to prolong it indefinitely without a new attack. It is, therefore, still the same note. But however little this action in pitch on the two edges of the sound is

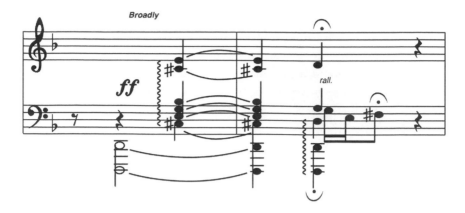

FIGURE 17. Example of a "large note" on the organ [in Bach].

The "inflation" of the first note is intended much more for its concrete effect than for the construction of a chord in the abstract.

FIGURE 18. Development of a "large note" [in a group].

clear or perceptible, this thick sound will produce two voices, as it were, with a confused zone between them that we can gradually efface. We will almost have produced a dichotomy. From this initial cell, from this one note, there will arise a melody and a countermelody, which will itself gradually modulate dynamically, i.e., be composed of elementary notes . . . So we move seamlessly from the "large note" to the group, and so we reverse the usual musical process that consists of creating groups with notes.

Let us now consider another example that also illustrates the concept of a musical object released from measured performance. This time concrete music instruments are not used to produce new structures, or an as yet unpublished way of developing these structures within one or several independent or correlated parameters. These instruments can also be used to create a polyphony or, more precisely, ensembles in which the various parts develop in accordance with given laws of synchronicity. One of these, the simplest, comes from "total transposition" i.e., a proportionality in reading speeds that transposes pitch and duration at the same time and in the same relationship with each other. I quite understand that a composition in keeping with these laws can be produced on paper, and accurately enough, using bar lines. But, apart from the fact that all Western music corresponds, ipso facto, to a metric beat, note by note and rhythm by rhythm, which makes such examples the exception, it is also the case that duple or triple time does not adapt well to such relationships, which always end up with some coincidence of fortes, some harmonic encounter, or some double bar line. In short, despite everything, it is difficult on the score to get rid of basic time, beaten time, the time that ultimately informs all our music. Conversely, we only have to set in motion three turntables, each with the same theme, at different speeds and we have a fugue in three voices, in tessitura, and in duration, absolutely rigorous, which has nothing to do with any composing or performing skill, but rather with the perfect suitability of machines for such performances.

What does an experiment like this give us? Of course, it all depends on whether the initial object, which is to be in fugue with itself, is well chosen or not, in matter or in form. We have composed fugues like this, entitled, perhaps too lightheartedly, *bidules* (thingumajigs). In the *Bidule en ut* (Thingumajig in C), for example, Pierre Henry at the piano and I at the turntable had chosen a theme halfway between pure and concrete music, with the result that the total transposition, slowing or speeding up an ensemble of quite rich matter, yielded interesting varieties of the same object and not a banal homothetic transformation. The resulting counterpoint appeared as entirely perceptible to the ear, which did perfectly well without the counterpoint of notes and could grasp the overall counterpoint of the objects as a whole. Better still, as the irrationality of the counterpoint, in the arithmetical sense of bars, was accompanied, it seems, by increasing rigor, both functionally and analytically, these

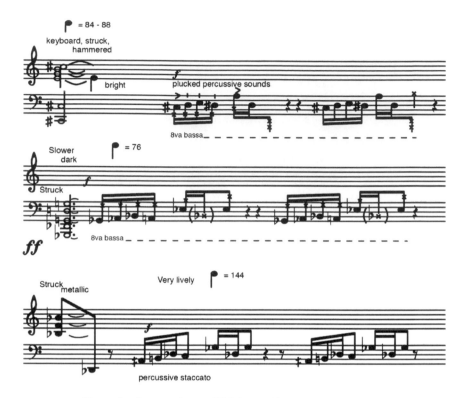

FIGURE 19. [Example of an autofugato *(Bidule en ut)*.]

short studies immediately aroused great interest and always gave musical pleasure, even though uninformed listeners were a long way from being able to analyze them immediately (fig. 19). One can see what a mistake it would be to decide, a priori, that an autofugue like this has no musical interest and leads only to tautology. This would be to judge according to the music of notes and not of objects. Now the latter, while remaining mathematically "like" themselves, change so much, acoustically and aesthetically, that even after listening two or three times a musician hesitates, not so much to analyze the various parts of the counterpoint, but to dare to recognize in it the three aspects of one and the same object.

Whereas the classical fugato relies on the metrical correspondence of the voices, note by note, independently of their tessitura, we can see that a new, well-tempered harpsichord could be composed based on the law of the correspondence between durations and tessituras. If we wished to be dogmatic, why should we not, like so many others, lay down a new law of the fugue? Why should we not employ psychologists to help us to demonstrate that in such total transpositions the human ear finds a balance of tempo that helps in listening to tessituras? It would indeed—if I may say so—be consonant with nature, and with its logarithmic laws, that the ear should like lower notes to be slower and higher notes to be faster. We might even, like Maurice Le Roux, support our case with a precedent—there are not many of them, it is true—taken from a famous text. For, after Maurice Le Roux had some dealings with concrete music, his intellectual curiosity in fact motivated him to seek out a number of precedents elsewhere. He had the good fortune to find a particularly convincing example in Berlioz (fig. 20). And so, in theory and in practice, we are opening up many avenues to researchers. Not only has the dead end been opened up, but this time the areas for exploration are so numerous that a great swarm of inventors appears to be needed. Everyone who wishes to undertake research into concrete music, provided he has some talent and a great deal of perseverance, can be sure that there, at least, he will be an innovator. No one yet really knows what a complex note is and what can be done with it, and the resources of total transposition, limited or otherwise, remain unexplored. But we are far from insisting on the rigorous use of the complex note. Rather, we would advise that it should be employed with discretion, guided above all by the ear, to see

FIGURE 20 *(overleaf)*. Example of a "total transposition" in classical music given by Maurice Le Roux (Berlioz, fifth part of the *Symphonie fantastique*).

> While a bell repeats an identical motif several times, as if to mark out the tempo, the theme of the Dies Irae is played at a very slow tempo by the two tubas and the bassoon and is then repeated by the horn and trombone at double tempo and tessitura, and finally four times faster by the (pizzicato) violins, while the tessitura is again doubled. There is therefore total transposition, not only in tempo and tessituras, but also, in a way, in timbres, as a result of the instrumental composition of each repeat.

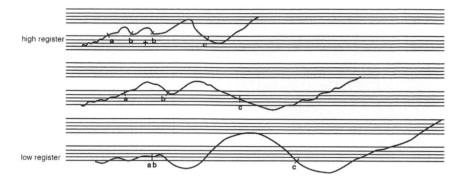

FIGURE 21. [Variations on the autofugue through transformations of the monophonies.]

to what extent the sound object being worked on is likely to be exhausted or to provide a resource. Why not, for example, introduce a transformation into the transposition? In figure 21 it can be seen that it is legitimate, for example, to introduce a cut in the bass repeat, or the replay of a segment in the treble repeat. Here no one will object that concrete music is formless. Its forms are sometimes too precise. The outlines of objects such as these are all the more rigorous for no longer being expressed in notes.

17 From the Object to Language

Looking at this seashell, in which I seem to see evidence of "construction" and, as it were, the work of a hand not operating by "chance," I wonder: *Who made it?*

This is the "way," indicated by Valéry, which leads, like a strait or an isthmus, from one world to another, from the world of found objects to the world of intended objects. The question of language does not arise immediately, and we would do well to stop here for the time being.

But soon my question changes. It penetrates further into the recesses of my simplicity, and now I strive to find out how we know that a given object is or is not *made by a man?*

Here, before the same object (a sound object, but the comparison with the seashell is perfectly adequate), there are two attitudes, depending on whether the observer is a specialist in seashells or not. The uninitiated will see the unexpected: "the most precious discoveries . . . ruin more often than affirm what we create from our own preferences: they are facts that are still *nonhuman,* that no imagination could have foreseen." The informed man, the seashell enthusiast, has observed, or reflected, to find out if "the idea of a certain form demanding from his mind I know not what capacity for similar forms" he were capable of imagining "how he might go about making a seashell." If he can, then the enthusiast realizes that he has understood this object. "I have explained it to myself through a series of my own acts, and thus have come to the end of my problem. Any attempt to go further would radically change it, and would lead me to deviate from explaining the seashell to explaining myself. Consequently, I may until now still consider that *this seashell is the work of a man.*" The authority of Valéry reassures us. When we say that choosing a sound object, being capable of knowing how it is made, and being able to reproduce it is already humanizing it, giving it the value of a musical structure, this is nothing other than repeating the gesture of the gatherer of seashells.

There follows the idea of comparing the found object with objects we already have. Here also there are two attitudes. The traditionalist observes that the new object has nothing in common with those in the collection. Suppose, for example, he has no system of reference for seashells but instead has a collection of marbles (they are indeed marbles if we think of the simplistic nature of classical musical structures), and suppose then that, considering the suitability of his marbles, and how they can be arranged in piles, in staggered rows, in nice rhythmical series, he finds the seashell too complicated and disparate and then considers that it has no meaning (or too many contradictory meanings) in comparison with his marbles, he rejects it: it does not, and could never have, meaning. However, the seashell enthusiast can turn the situation around. First he can ask what the marbles enthusiast sees, and how, in his marbles. Valéry, observing that the marble enthusiast can do only one thing and in one way, comments that "this thing does itself as it were, and therefore its action is not really human (as no thought at all is required), and we do not understand it." And so we have tried to show that it could be the same with music. We know how to make music, but do we understand it? The seashell can be abandoned if we prefer the simplicity of marbles. But the shell, an object given by nature, can teach us more about man than marbles, which we have played around with far too much. Hence, as I wrote in the program for the first concrete music concert, might it be the object that has something to say to us? This something, if we go along with Valéry, would be essentially human, for "our deliberate designs and our willed constructions or handiworks seem very far removed from *our deepest organic activity.*"

Since we are referring so much to this author, let us go on from *L'homme et la coquille* (The man and the seashell) and, without leaving *Variété V* (Variety V), turn to *Poésie et pensée abstraite* (Poetry and abstract thought). This is to find an answer to the following difficulty: the seashell enthusiast takes up the object and this object says something to him, but how can he use it to communicate with others? It all revolves around a word, and an idea: Is music a language? Let us immediately put aside the misunderstanding caused by the definition. If every series of objects gathered together, classified, and used by man to communicate with his peers is by definition a language, everything will be language: the stones of monuments, the painter's colors, the cinema screen, everything. Suppose we accept this convention of . . . language. We still immediately have to distinguish two languages, or, more precisely, language used in two worlds, prose and poetry. We shall limit ourselves to referring, apart from Valéry and Souriau, to Paulhan, and Parrain, among many others, to show that the two uses of language are firmly accepted, depending on whether it is used as sign and meaning, or as signal or substance. In the one case it acts as a factor in a relationship; in the other it has full autonomy. In effect, the former use takes from the substance of language the minimum necessary for its meaning to be transmitted; the other use involves the concrete aspect of language, i.e., all the psycho-sensorial elements contained in the phenomenon of language and all the potential for expression it contains.

One of the pitfalls of any phenomenology of music arises precisely from the fact that music is quoted by almost all authors—and particularly by those I have named—to explain the second use of language. Valéry, for example, says, "Every word is the instantaneous combination of a *sound* and a *meaning*, which have absolutely no connection with each other." This is only one step away from saying that since the sound of a word indicates precisely its poetic content, music is itself one aspect of poetic language. And many mistakes arise from this. On the contrary, it must be clearly understood that the same distinction between prose and poetry emerges in almost all—doubtless, in all—the arts. If we carefully consider the differences between figurative and abstract painting, we shall have to agree that the first, which concerns resemblance with the subject, is mainly plastic prose, which acts as a sign, whereas in the other, forms and colors, with no reference to anything, demand to signify in themselves and to express everything that is potentially contained in their "signal." And what about music?

If the contribution made by the concrete experiment in music has been clearly understood, it will not be difficult to see that although classical music is indeed a language, it is a language used more as prose than as poetry. Indeed, every musical note, like words, has a *sound* and a *meaning*. A C on the trumpet is, on the one hand, a sound that musicians are quite incapable of analyzing and using as such, and it is also a collection of abstract qualities, selected by a deliberate choice of the mind (after passing rapidly and almost insignificantly through the sensorial ear). The trumpet is, I agree, a persona got up as a trumpet, but whose responsibility is basically to say the word "C" in an established dialogue while he, or others, continue the discourse. People will say, "We know what you're getting at. You want us to hear the trumpet as such, to recognize the persona first, and think 'trumpet' and not 'C.'" Wrong, wrong again! If you think "trumpet" you are still stuck in language; you have gone through another door, even more prosaic, which this time leads to music heard as a "language of things," the twin brother, though out of favor, a homonymic though deponent form of the language of words. If you perceive "trumpet" you make the utterance of the word through the intermediary of the sound "trumpet," and the sound phenomenon can do nothing other than to *signify* the object trumpet. The sound of the trumpet simply names the object. By a strange paradox of habit, here man is no longer in direct contact with the concrete; the process of abstraction (and particularly the causal relationship) immediately comes into play and wholly masks the object. People may adduce as counterargument the automatic associations triggered by the sound of the trumpet: warriors, historic stories . . . But these associations are all contained in the utterance of the word-object. So if prose is superseded here, it is because of the poetry of words and not the poetry of the sound object. So when does the phenomenon of musical poetry occur? When the ear perceives an unusual sound object, absolutely distinct, both in musical language, represented by C, and in the language of things that underlies the word and the object "trumpet." Neither musical sound nor noise, the pure musical object gives access, doubtless for the first time, to the domain of musical poetry.

The prose-poetry distinction does not reside only in the two accepted meanings of one relationship. It also arises from two ways of using them, and the effectiveness of one or the other. Poetry first arose, it would seem, out of play. Man, who in order to live and subsist must have rapidly put together sign-alphabets, or simply manipulated objects, assembled solids, used his limbs, perceives that they can be used gratuitously and with absolutely no apparent purpose. Prose and poetry then begin to be dissociated in many fields. Walking has a double, which is dance. Writing and drawing for utilitarian purposes also have doubles: the mystic sign, figurative drawing, which itself found a double in abstract art, etc. . . . For a long time this poetic option was considered as an entertainment, made for pleasure, for dreaming, or was directed away from its gratuitousness toward more august, but still in a sense utilitarian, goals: this is the case with dance, sign, and incantation used in religion. And then a sort of seesawing over different periods occurs, depending on whether they tend toward the prosaic or the poetic in the use of signs. They are prosaic if they are perfectly satisfied with the conventional signs they use: if not, the sign becomes vague, loses content, and people become attached to its form, its shape, much more than to the meaning it was supposed to have. In classical periods, for example, poetry in effect disappears. Although in the Middle Ages there was a verbal poetry, a music vague enough to sometimes be poetic, the seventeenth century has nothing more poetic left than the horse, which lost its big toe for the sake of having one hoof. The tragedies of Corneille and Voltaire are not poems;

the music of Lully is only discourse, language as sign triumphs. That the language is rhymed and in alexandrines, and that its crafting attains a certain mastery, I do not dispute, but these are secondary characteristics. Language borrows poetry as a train borrows rails. Alexandrines in the seventeenth century are no more than a railway prosody: rails twelve feet long, rhyme-bell, we travel along all the better; all the meaning is in the discourse. Because, extremely subtle, infinitely refined, the poetic aspect of alexandrine prose seduces us into thinking, let us be in no doubt, academically or through an excess of imagination, that language is being used poetically. When does this occur? It recurs, for good or ill, when, in the words of H. Michaux, "words are directed away from their author's flock," and when the author not only agrees but organizes everything for this betrayal. A discourse determined, not humbly marked out, by rhyme, assonances in which words are associated by their sound rather than their meaning, these are the unmistakable (perhaps regrettable) symptoms of the phenomenon of poetry in language. Then, from here to verbal surrealism, from the aptly named Monsieur Sully Prudhomme to the Prévert of the *Dîner de Têtes* (Masked dinner) via more serious inhabiters of the poetic adventure, like Verlaine or Rimbaud, there is not long to wait, and only a little seriousness to be shed. Why do I say quite at random Verlaine and Rimbaud if not because I am unconsciously choosing two completely contrasting poets, one who believed in words and one who, no longer believing in them, did not even experience the sweetness of an alcoholic, yet nevertheless literary, end? Well, now words are being worn down to the point of lettrism, since, in the space of a few years, as if in one huge hemorrhage, the surrealists have exhausted the sounds of words. (As can be seen, poetry is simply letting oneself go with the flow.) What will be left for the latecomers? When Jean Tardieu takes one word for another, when Queneau does exercises in style, can we not see a final and perhaps mortal convulsion of verbal poetry? The adventures of bus "S" are indubitably prose, but prose that catches poetry in the net of a syntax and pitfalls from one object to another. As for Jean Tardieu, *Mot pour un autre* (Word for another) is the height of poetic license, but this entire poem amounts to no more than telling little stories in comical prose. So it seems with these two *latest* poets that the line is finished, and poets, just like musicians, are declaring that they will soon be out of work, or are having to join some university department that we hope will soon be open, and which Brice Parrain is about to define, of experimental language.

It is not, therefore, purely a whim or some vague intuition of mine that led me to open the doors of the concrete music studio both to poets breaking with verbal language and to musicians breaking away from melody. On the condition, perhaps, that they are joined and helped by several specialists in the plastic arts (good at the abstract) and several sound engineers (craftsmen in concrete sound), an uncharted territory is being opened up in this place, but in any case we must say good-bye to any sign of intelligence, any resemblances, any known words, any notes, any conventional figures, and so to any form of language. In short, the musical object is getting ready to take over the word at the end of this race for poetry.

These latest conclusions and wishes are not without some contradiction with other conclusions, other wishes I expressed above, that my hope for concrete music was that it would not be without links with language in general, and with musical discourse in particular. Is there a way out of this contradiction, and any hope for me in this quandary, which has so often torn me apart over all these last years in the studio?

To find an answer to a question like this, this time I am obliged to move into a field that I feel to be less certain, and where people will want to see more personal commitment, signs of an avowed liking, whereas it seems to me that the preceding paragraphs could be objectively corroborated and apply to all who are tempted by—and who attempt—the adventure of concrete music.

I have always been surprised by the difference of my musical tastes, and by the fact that, independently of how my musical culture has developed, I remain relatively unresponsive to Mozart, whereas my fervor for Bach never ceases to grow. This has made me ask myself questions on this subject, especially the use, by Bach or Mozart, of a particular musical language. I am sorry to have to bring in such irreproachable masters, and I would have preferred to carry out my analysis on lesser ones. However, compared to expressionism, which I disapprove of more and more in music (while still remaining very responsive to a Schumann, for example), they guarantee that I shall remain within the pale. I mean that before the Romantics, musical discourse is used with exemplary dignity. It never explicitly involves sadness or elation. Too bad about Beethoven, who attracts me less and less. I like the way that, in Bach as well as in Mozart, the same phrase, the same theme, can communicate both the most human pity and the most inaccessible joy; I am grateful that, if these composers indicate a feeling, they do it not in relation to their personal state of mind but in relation to the reason for their music, which often lies its destination, sacred or secular, its circumstances, ceremonial or informal, and is also often dictated by a specific text.

Others may be grateful to Beethoven for opening up the floodgates of the heart, making the quartet into a tool of intimacy, the kettledrum into an appeal, so moving that it can be used 150 years later as the radio signature for nations at war; it would be difficult to see an extract from a work by Mozart or Bach used for warlike or sentimental purposes. Beethoven showed the way to everything that was to become, more and more, musical rhetoric. And we do not even need to mention the deviations of music toward an explicitness where it loses its way—symphonic poems, songs without words, or dubious lyrical ensembles that occupied so much of the stupid nineteenth century. It can be seen that this use of music, taking it further and further away from the creation of a perfect object, turns it more and more into common currency; if, as the Greek philosophers hoped, music had a chance of spelling out to human beings the language of the gods, men were ceaselessly going to make it speak the most human of languages, and, on the pretext of refining their feelings, the most devoid of interest. For, after all, men have many, and much more efficient, ways of communicating with each other. They have very few, as far as we know, of communicating collectively with a universe that is beyond them and is not besmirched with anthropomorphism. Mozart and Bach have in common that they speak a language that we can still believe to be the language of the gods.

But Mozart talks too much for my liking, and too clearly. I should, if such lèse majesté were allowed, accuse him of being chatty and superficial, simplistic. Insofar as he gives us an object that is too facile, without internal contradiction, and which, even though it may not be tied to a banal expressionism, nevertheless expresses a satisfaction with linear development, I cease to be interested or moved. In other words, Mozart, though he serves music well, shuts himself inside it and encloses us with him. He constructs a closed world; he is a sort of tautology. If, with Bach, I feel not only music but music as a microcosm, a fragment of the world, a sphere that is both within and without man, this is because Bach's constructions take on so many contradictions and counterarguments, such flagrant inner tensions and at the same time such serenity in the strife, that I can both rest and find comfort in him, and Bach's music does not close in on itself or on me like a prison: it is an open world, an image of the universe.

Where does such a difference come from, technically speaking? Can it be explained? One would have to be a better musician than I to say. May I, without ridicule, put forward some suggestions? It seems to me, personally, that Mozart is entirely grounded in what I would call the "note-by-note," the word-by-word, rhetoric. Perfectly clear exposition, development, conclusion. Someone is talking to me, and, while he charms everything around him, all he does for me is to impose his chatter. Bach's voices arise, and it does not matter what each of them says: I respond to their speech. It is in more than the universe of the dominant that these voices move, these trajectories are followed. The trajectories are scarcely important. I will even say that I care very little whether the chosen theme is beautiful; much more I marvel that rigorous yet half-hidden relationships are established among these trajectories. Limited to the universe of the dominant, they nevertheless show what connections are possible and how in all probability these can be generalized across the entire universe, musical or otherwise. It is doubtless the same with a particular use of language, of all language, by particular geniuses. Some, in their use of language, remain within. Their work is, as it were, of no effect and in any case limited to their sphere of expression. Others get past this obstacle and, in the same way that physicists use the same symbols to go beyond these symbols, and their *imagination* to imagine the inconceivable, they create "open worlds," worlds involving some universal scheme for all reality.

What I am getting at is doubtless clearer. A Mozart type of music is absolutely no good to us in concrete music. Mozart's simple structure, used for its own sake, is no longer relevant. Bach's style of music can never cease to instruct us. It is the relationships between the structures that count and will doubtless, transposed, remain. Indeed, movements to the dominant perhaps no longer have any place in concrete music. But the relationships between one object and another always have a place. Here it is no longer even a question of poetry. Poetry perhaps plays the same role for language as the philosopher for thought. We use these words, poetry, philosophy, to designate an absence of rigor, highly desirable if the aim is to prefigure, or highly regrettable if it is playing on words, or with ideas. Poetry and philosophy are reservoirs of expectation, the limbo of a sufficient language or of more daring disciplines of thought. A *Gestalttheorie* is merely a new word in a philosophical jargon, or should announce a new science, which involves its own method. To apply such a scientific approach to the study of Bach, for example, is not profanity; it is rigorously applying the whole man (and not only his intellect: his heart, his thinking muscles) to that musical object of great stature, in order to see in it both a more general music and something else more far-reaching than music. Such laws, once glimpsed, would be the true key to the relationships between object and object, and between subject and object.

If the object has something to say to us, it will not be through worn-out words, clapped-out symbols squeezed of all their savor. It will be like the stars or atoms whose whole poetry is in a new rigor in understanding.

18 From the Object to the Subject

The wave of curiosity that gave us the seashell object recedes and leaves us face to face. Nature bestows her gifts and makes no comment. So man— and our contemporaries give many examples of this—behaves with the waywardness of a young animal. He immediately leaves off what he was doing and runs after his new find. I am afraid of being too successful. If some people deny me the notion of the object, being too passionately attached in music to a communication that they consider immediate between two "subjects," thereby dodging the object that they use as intermediary, I am afraid, I say, that newcomers may take hold of the object and think only about it, not knowing, or pretending not to know, that someone makes it, or at least defines and chooses it, and that someone becomes aware of it, or at least experiences it and is, in some more or less mysterious and more or less rudimentary way, impressed by it.

I would only really be at peace with myself if the concrete approach succeeded, at least initially, in isolating a particular objective zone in music, making the sound object, the way it is perceived and made, into a proper subject for inquiry, that is, for analysis and experimentation. And if, furthermore, it succeeded in making minds receptive to those two symmetrical relationships that obtain between the object and the two "subjects," the one active (in principle), the other passive (ditto), which use the object either to communicate—as in a language—or more simply and more mysteriously still, to communicate in one and the same encounter.

I fear that here I may meet two types of minds that, although not conservative and both adherents of the scientific method, are nonetheless closed to my new question. The first will say that everything is language; there is no question of a direct relationship between subject and object. The same old relativist arguments: the use of an object by man is nothing but a convention. The others, turning their backs on the former, allowing that one informs the other, will plug the human body into a galvanometer and will start to treat man like a frog. Bringing to his ear sounds of a concrete nature now devoid of all poetry, they will measure, like Pavlov's dog, his output of saliva or the contraction of his muscles. This is not a fanciful notion on my part: biologists have already started. They have discovered that the "impedance" of the human body, determined in general by attentiveness, presents variations due to auditory stimulation. From here to drawing up a list of sounds measured in psycho-galvanic megohms is but a short step; as the impedance of the human body would itself be physically altered by the secretions from the sweat glands, laws between musical impressions and the secretion of sweat would be established. And then what?

At a concert I watch a respectable Gentleman, a correct Lady. I assume that the music in the program is of the kind that will kindle euphoric behavior in them. The gentleman's shoe, the lady's boot, may well soon be synchronized with the conductor's baton, all the more so as the conductor, a man of generally undeniable fame, is understood to be a magisterial metronome, a master oscillator. The same people will smile and, depending on their degree of liberalism, be touched by the spectacle, perhaps brought to them by Technicolor, of those wonderful Africans at their drums. They are assured of possessing the authentic elixir of an immaculate spirituality in their music: meanwhile, innocent and uncontrolled, a little boot taps away, revealing all . . .

Meanwhile, what is the other *subject* doing? Up in his box, not far from the pines immortalized by Respighi, surrounded with pencils and erasers—who knows whether he chews them frantically, whether, like every undergraduate in an examination, he sticks out a tongue, the length of which would be avidly measured by the watching biologist if only he could experiment as he wished? What are other composers doing, those who don't know they are composers, and who, moreover, don't know that they are indeed composing whole scores of concrete music? Those adolescents, lovers of onomatopoeia, who imitate Native American drumrolls or react to a show, an event, or communicate their inner vision, their state of mind, to their mates with labials, plosives, hoarse whispers, the smacking of lips, the sucking-in of cheeks, catcalls, thigh slapping? Are they thinking of movements to the dominant, or six-eight time? Of course not. No movement to the dominant, no rational rhythm can adequately exteriorize such muscular states of mind. It is not only the larynx that by its contractions prefigures melody.[1] The rib cage, the thighs, the tongue also have a *plan* known only to them. Man has more that is sonorous than a voice, more than vocal cords ready for sound. Through his throat he aspires to perfect numbers, and Pythagoras is his crowning glory, but his whole body is involved in the stimuli of his ear and subhears other sounds that may not belong to the scale. In the same way that there is an "inner melody," there may be an intimation in the human body of a concrete music in embryo.

When Montherlant gives a chapter in *Relève du matin* (Morning watch) the title "Le chant profond" (The song deep within), when Charles Lalo uses the word "inner song" in a very specific sense in his *Eléments*

---

1. This is not a figure of speech. It has been demonstrated that when a melody was being listened to, the larynx contracted and ghosted the sounds of the melody without emitting any sound. This is due to a general law of the psychology of sensations: "All images tend to be expressed through a movement" (cf. Ch. Lalo, *Eléments d'une esthétique musicale scientifique*) (Elements of a scientific aesthetics of music).

d'esthétique musicale scientifique when, in a recent conversation, François Le Lionnais confides his faith in a secret correspondence between musical forms and forms written deep within the heart of man, then we really must acknowledge a convergence. As a result of a chain reaction going from the most sensory to the most spiritual and using the most material or muscular means of expression, the subject attunes to the object. Music is of particular interest because it is without a doubt one of the only areas in which the chain reaction is so extensive and goes so far in linking together worlds that without it would be closed and sealed. What are we to make of musicians who are wholly occupied either with the object or with one or another of the subjects, and who thus refuse what is most exciting in the phenomenon of music?

So the object is at the center of the chain, and it could be said that it raises a question about awareness rather than facture. How is the object made? How is it perceived? The second question again belongs to the *how* of science; an answer could be found by putting the various specialties to work: from the biologist to the psychologist, from the historian to the philologist, from the ethnologist to the acoustician, there is much to be done, and especially to ensure their work is not carried out in a vacuum, with no links between them. If the specialists are left to their own devices, there will be interesting studies about music—biological, psychological, historical, ethnological, etc.—but as music is the very thing that links them, and as it is the thing that links them that should be the subject of a new field of study, there is every probability that the aforementioned specialists will miss the essential.

The study of music should therefore be first and foremost the study of a relationship, the double relationship between the object and the subject. It is no surprise that this field of study lags behind other well-defined specialties. This is the general situation and affects nearly all modern disciplines, so much so that, if this gap is to be filled, it may be that this can only be done through the creation of a new specialty. Only a specialist in *relationship* would dare to build bridges from one specific field to another. Cybernetics, a term that is still obscure to the public, seems to be a discipline of this type. So what is cybernetics? According to Norbert Wiener, its founder, it is "the theory of communications and control in living beings, as well as in societies and machines." Naturally—and this is characteristic of the civilization to which we have the honor to belong— man is always the ill-shod cobbler. Although such a theory has applications vital to his happiness, the happiness of the societies he forms, the understanding of his inner world, he starts with machines. It is machines, their behavior, that first arouse his attention. See him, impelled by a utilitarianism that could well be considered sordid, wondering about machines he himself has made, as if they suddenly appeared to him like outlandish beings brought to him by nature and which must be discovered and tamed. What more delightful reversal of the situation than that this study of machines, viewed as beings, should move him to inquire more deeply into himself? What a triumph, not of materialism, but, because of and through the most radically materialistic means, of a return to a certain type of spirituality, composed of greater clarity, and a mystery brought to full enlightenment! Now, it is not difficult to see in the use of cybernetics for an understanding of man by man a phenomenon that runs parallel to what we saw as a probability in music. When man creates machines, he creates them by following not his inner music but his inner mechanism. How could he invent machines that are not, in some way, more or less successful and always partial replicas of himself? If he turns to machines, seen as beings in their own right, will he not be better placed to discover, magnified and caricatured, certain properties of his own nature, which Nature, having buried them too deeply or made them too complex, rendered impenetrable? So why should the study of music appear so different from the study of man, and why should there be only a superficial relationship of convention and language between subject and object, whereas there is everything to hope for in an, infinitely more probable, hypothesis that there is intrinsic correspondence?

If this is so, we can see what avenues, both classical and modern, are opened up by this way of thinking. The expressionism of musical decadence is countered by an objective impressionism. Bringing it to light has nothing to do with words. A falsely explanatory language could not possibly exhaust a phenomenon that needs to be felt rather than named. If music is a language, then it is a specific language. There is no more a parallel between music and speech than between sound and light. Sound and light bring us different categories of information. Intelligence and heart open up to us complementary worlds, which are not opposed but cannot be dissociated. So music should remain within itself, like a fully current language in a classical period, and *serve.*

And so, after the *how,* and in our endeavor to find an answer to the how, we come to the *why* of music, and perhaps we shall be able to find an answer. Why music? Because it is not only useful but necessary for an understanding of the world, and of man. Here I fear that a skillful shift in argument may lead people to agree too easily. Introduced in another way, a question like this would have brought about a denial or a shrug of the shoulders. If, for example, I had asked if music was a completely disinterested Art, or if it should be put to some useful purpose, I would easily have aroused indignation. Now I have just solicited assent to the contrary. So it is important that we understand each other.

And indeed I have in mind the reactions to concrete music at the discussion in Aix at UNESCO. This session, under the heading "Humanism and Music," was supposed to tackle the question of the destination of music in the deepest sense. You can imagine the resultant cacophony. The vaguest approximations, the most sentimental expressionism, were given free rein. Music, come on? Communication with the infinite, Joy with a capital J, said some. Others, more moderate, sought a historical justification for it, a civilizing process with a birth certificate, probably Greek, and in a specific century. And so, in the blink of an eye, they went from the vaguest idealist justification to highly contingent historical precision . . . Then one of the delegates was pleased to point out that Music, *in former times,* arose from the sacred, and since then it had greatly lost out. This comment, vague and gratuitous though it was, received no opposition. What were these former times, this sacred, and in what respect could music have declined? Who cared! This origin was immediately welcomed by the right thinking. And there was the same unanimity, this time in condemning so-called "functional" music, piped to factory workers with the miserable aim of increasing their productivity. This without reservation. And what if, for example, in the course of tedious labors that only occupy the hands while minds wander off—into the pathetic world of boredom and inner impoverishment—it were possible to listen to some music (maybe, as far as the employers were concerned, for purposes that were not disinterested), and the worker's inner life or merely his pleasure were nevertheless enhanced by this? Who cares about these details? It is so much easier for right-thinking international delegates to pass a resolution unanimously condemning outright all music saddled with the infamous (and stupid) name of functional . . . The same assembly raises its hat to Gregorian chant, is cheered by the thought of the monks who sang it, without even wondering if the reasons for this music lie precisely in the fact that it is functional in a higher sense?

In any case, what these Western musicians do, for the most part, agree about is a number of limitations: the intellectual limitations of a music cut off from the concrete and the senses, as we have pointed out often enough; historical and geographical limitations, as we have mentioned; but also the limitation, implicit and contradictory, of the function of music to a dubious, scarcely acknowledged aestheticism.

Indeed, at one moment they hark back to the Grand Siècle definition, when the whole of Art was to please, and at another they evoke a vaguely mystical—or rather, to my mind, a vulgarly emotional—sensibility. If it's Bach, they allude to the spiritual; if it's black music they exclude it. And so they create a gulf—for what reason, in the name of what bundle of muscles or nerves aroused in different ways?—between the sacred according to Bach and the sacred according to Tabou. Meanwhile, the sons and daughters of the same right-thinking people, under their very noses, copy the black musicians. If they dance in cellars, and with such passion, it is perhaps because there is more that is human, or more that is divine— in any case, there is more fervor and instinctive warmth, in a word, more *point*—in hot jazz than in the music of the Prix de Rome.

Let us return to the example of Bach and see how the subject-object relationship develops. Even when we have accepted that good intentions do not make an artist, and that from the beginning there must be genius, how can we imagine Bach's work without a religious context? Because Bach is depicted as a good family man churning out his cantata every Sunday, does this mean that he isn't a mystic? On the contrary, miracle workers and seers have always come from the common herd and have had the strongest constitutions. We would happily project our own weaknesses, our brokenness, onto the extraordinary works of a Bach; we would have him a genius on the one hand, a mystic on the other. We find it hard to imagine that here the two are one, that Bach directly expresses his mysticism in the musical object, and that this and his technical skill are one and the same. When Bach juggles with the voices in a fugue; when, in a rigorous universe watched over by the four cardinal points of the dominant, like archangels, he builds structures and forms; when he calculates how they attract and repel, I like to think that Bach, both architect and priest, is meditating in four voices, revealing the identity of the human and the divine, and participating in an incarnation mystery.

Conversely, how can we hear Bach except by taking on this dualism, or, more precisely, by striving, for a few privileged moments and because of his work, to resolve our latent dualism? If a bad musician listens to Bach he will not manage to enter into the edifice. All that will come to him is a vague halo of sound, as if this domain were alien to him. A man with a perfect sense of harmony who analyzes the cantatas coldly and without feeling, without a window onto the world of faith, will merely be contemplating dead stones. There is no real cathedral without prayer. Oh! Truly, music is not just an entertainment.

Really—and here we come back to Valéry—the listener cannot know an object unless he is capable of reproducing it, making it as if for the first time. Bach should be listened to in this spirit: this requires not just profound knowledge, but spiritual preparation.

I have chosen Bach not for ease of presentation, but in order to benefit from a certain favor, a certain credit that is given to music when it attains such heights. But I still have to say how the relationship can function in other, less sublime examples. We have seen that Bach's work presupposes a civilization, technical skill, and also a worldview. These conditions suit some individuals. It is a pity that the whole of humanity cannot have access to them, but we have to accept that this is how it is. Why not see the same phenomenon, to a lesser degree, and only partially, in all musics? African music very clearly appeals more to the guts than the intellect, to the "red brain." Instead of giving a variation of the object, the permanence of forms gives the subject an inner journey through the repetition of the object. Has this been sufficiently recognized? Whether this journey is vulgar, or it points exclusively to certain goals (eroticism, violence), have people seen the importance of considering music in its subjective reality?

The shock that we, as a listener much more than an author, felt when faced with the first concrete music objects brought us very suddenly up against these basic truths. There is, after all, a certain arrogance in listening to a sound object and expecting it to develop. Have we really listened to it? What visceral, or muscular, or neural level has it reached? Through using and abusing this type of listening, our whole psychological makeup may become disturbed. Some sounds may make us ill, and our experiments have not been without effects on our health. We were expecting sounds from concrete music, the continuation of a familiar game, the application of age-old rules. The object resists, it won't play, it sets into a wearisome sameness, it imposes. And this is the stage we're at. By doing this, the object forces us to listen to it, not by reference, but just as it is, in all the reality of its substance. As it doesn't say much, and certainly not what we would like it to say, once we have heard it, it makes us fall silent. In this silence we perceive new disturbances. It isn't only the larynx, whose contractions, according to Stricker, ghost the melody. The secret sound penetrates us, extending into disturbing and profoundly hidden realms beyond. This immediately gives rise to associations that are contradictory, confused and varied enough to make us have to admit that communication between author and listener is based on total misunderstanding. It is at this point that we must ask whether we are still dealing with a language, and whether concrete music, even willed, should strive to say something. Maybe, by constructing series along the lines of previous, more or less successfully generalized, intellectualist schemes, we are turning our back on a possible future. Maybe it is our instinctual onomatopoeia that should be seeking an outlet in constructions that would result in more visceral musics. By unleashing a chaos of concrete sounds we are at least assured of one response; we strike terror, we arouse anguish. Young authors like nothing so much as that and have not yet enough human experience to be careful with mankind, and to bother about what they put into circulation. I do want a visceral music, but I don't want it to be just violence and bodily disorder. Moreover, most of all I dread the opposite: that an excess of intellectualism not tempered by instinct might produce effects that will themselves trigger anguish, and anguish alone. A welter of sounds like this, very much in keeping with the times, it is true, would be only yet another example of mankind not up to the job, the apprentice surpassed by his sorcery. I have little interest in success at this price. I urge composers of concrete music, if there are any, not to unleash anything and everything, and not to be just anyone churning out just anything. And to think about who will be helped or harmed by their work.

19 Inventory

The man who, through more or less fortuitous circumstances, feels as if
he has broken free from the times he lives in and has reached open country is not a little surprised to find other fugitives moving around him
some years later. That forest, those trees, which he thought lifeless, are
indeed, as in *Macbeth,* other adventurers disguised as plant life. Should
he stop moving forward, our precursor will find himself in the rear guard.
From being ahead of his time, he becomes all the more a part of it, and,
after being part of the first wave, he now merely serves as a facilitator for
those that follow.

This sort of surprise, it is true, happens mostly to self-taught men,
who are usually more or less solitary, or in any case uncultured enough.
If they were more worldly-wise, would they have had that naïve curiosity that carries discovery innocently along, in an embryogenesis that, a

posteriori, seems a mite ridiculous as it is already out of date? . . . "But
So-and-So had already done that in 1924! . . ." the aesthete on duty will
say. Blessed ignorance of some who, unaware of this, have had a chance
of going further by trying. Unfortunate knowledge, which is not know-
how, of others, who are eaten away by snobbery. Indeed by a double
snobbery: snobbery that makes much of the very latest discovery and
despises the technique, the means. A naïve admiration is given to the results, while the process, plain for all to see, is nonetheless not perceived
in itself. Someone puts handlebars on a bicycle saddle and we're all carried away with admiration. The gesture is bold, true, particularly if we
see a plan for the future in it. But the gesture is also childlike; it comes
from elementary psychology, and it is no less interesting to consider it as
such. It could simply be a joke. Sometimes I am surrounded by musicians
who don't like music any more. The bias toward the completely unheard
gets on their nerves. "Grids," in reality very simplistic, and "parameters,"
of which they have only just grasped the definition, make them believe
that they are engaging with scholarly music, whereas in reality they are
simply pursuing the outcome, which, alas! is all too unheard. As long as
I retain only the procedure, technical or intellectual, that underlies all
this machinery and am prepared to denounce its systematic nature or
any blind application of it, I am snubbed. Everyone is for rigor, and above
all for avoiding any sound that might suggest something. The pursuit of
the record for the unheard is under way; the race is full on. People are
grateful to me for this one thing, for giving pedals to these cyclists. They
are disappearing into the fog.

By one of the most curious paradoxes I have ever been given to experience, I am witnessing this: I put forward an experimental approach in
music, which involves a scientific method. This method, as we know, is
constantly to police the method by the outcome. And now I find before
me two categories of musician: classical, for whom this approach is against
nature, and who are frightened by the idea of experimenting on sounds
without producing an immediately intelligible work; and the others,
who burst into the studio and, on the pretext of experimentation, rush
headlong into theory, demand bar lines, and ape the engineers. Putting
numbers in the place of sounds, measuring them to an eighth of a tone,

or the semidecibel, or the centimeter, fills them with confidence. They muddle disciplines. They were invited into a specific experimental method, i.e., to make a contribution within the rigorous framework of musical objectivity. They rush into an algebra of sounds, a combinatorial analysis of the pure object. My God, I've asked often enough for the musical object to be taken into account. Surely I have the right to ask as well for the subject to play its part. An experimental method in music means *listening:* first of all, all the time, before, during, after. Because the object is strange, courage lies in going on to define its humanity and beauty, in seeking reassurance not by pursuing the kilometric path, the white pebbles of measurement, but because we have used our taste, made a choice. Because also, for years, we have had the honesty to reject found objects if they are ugly or poisonous. Because we will go to the lengths of burning our furniture if at last we find a varnish that is purer and above all more durable.

However, what else is going on around us? Several signs indicate that the whole forest is on the move; chance encounters are putting us in contact with our next-door neighbors. There is perhaps nothing so exciting for a discoverer as to meet, on his own ground, and with absolutely nothing to cause it, the neighbor who is interested in similar things in quite different ways, and after a journey that is more unexpected on each occasion. John Cage has put screws into his piano. If I say that he did this almost without thinking, it isn't a criticism. He seems to me to be a clever Columbus who, fascinated by the first island, has built himself an exquisite villa on it. Varèse has devoted himself to that poor relation of the orchestra, the drum set. He has promoted it into an orchestra. Here and there he has added several effects from American studios. I don't know the details. More or less electronic kazoos, roaring sounds fabricated I don't know how, but occasionally similar in every respect to ours. Varèse crosses France without a stopover. This Frenchman has not had our good fortune of being a prophet in his own country. He is awaited and honored in Germany. Then he will go back to New York, where he is considered a master. Oddly, Varèse, who, though improving the orchestra, has always used it, and who does not prepare the piano like Cage, composes music that sometimes strangely resembles concrete music. The Germans, for their part, have really let electronics loose on sounds. They have gone further than the desire to rethink timbres; they are encroaching on the "body of the note" and play percussion noises in low frequencies. Their effects are occasionally close to ours, clearer and yet more impoverished. All these neighbors have in common that they are seeking to rethink the instrumental means that give them a sound material in which we recognize several of our objects. They do not seem to have had our eureka moment. They are still "playing" music, music in which the instrument informs their whole composition. The instrument still hides the object from them. They are getting very warm in this game of hunt the object and are almost there, but they haven't yet got their hands on it.

Maurice Martenot devotes the fruits of modern research to what is most traditional in music: no electronic equipment more honors the musical note; none approaches it with more respect, subtlety, clarity. How easy it is to recognize men by their works, whether they are inventions of steel, or waves, or electrons! Ondes Martenot are the very stuff of honesty and respect for classical music. What leeway was there still in classical music? Timbre. Maurice Martenot has carved out a masterly field of study here, giving composers a keyboard that, incidentally, they do not know how to use. It is probable that, after concrete music, when it has gone too far, people will go back to the ondes Martenot, which hadn't gone far enough: series based on the concept of the complex note, which the equipment of concrete music is separating out from the dross, can be made with the ondes Martenot, series that are limited, it is true, but that leave quite a good margin between the classical and the complex note.

In reality, it is quite easy to explain the rather limited interest that has been shown in electronic instruments in general, and in the ondes Martenot in particular. It was too much or too little. Too much for those who remained within traditional music, where timbre is not a parameter but ultimately merely serves to distinguish the voices of the polyphony. There are enough instruments for this, and they have the advantage of being classical. Not enough for those who wanted to use everything that the new instrument provided: to make full use of its richness of timbre, to make timbre a dimension of music, you have to leave pitch music behind. Once the traditional orchestra has gone, ondes Martenot are waiting for a new orchestra to take them on and use them. I congratulate myself for not having used the ondes until now; what further misunderstanding we would have caused ourselves! A more established science of the use of timbre in relation to pitch, and of the complex note in general, will probably enable the ondes to develop and find a new use.

And here, a warning: I hope that new enthusiasts of concrete music will heed me. Faced with new instruments, they too are going to want to *play* them. What if these instruments were not, or not yet, instruments for playing music? What if they were instruments first and foremost for analysis, and aids for the creative imagination? That would be odd. Why haven't I got the Prix de Rome! Perhaps I might leave my own inventions aside for the moment and, armed with a new concept of sounds, go back to the orchestra and write, for the orchestra (which can just about accommodate concrete experimentation), scores that would have no connection with either the dominant or atonality.

Or else, to the extent that *phonogènes* provide irreplaceable sound objects, I could take some element from them, but I would be sure to make them fit in with the orchestra. Why not indeed make the orchestra responsible for the development of this uncouth, blunt, brutish, almost unmanageable object? We would refer back to the example in chapter 16 on the "large note": a bridge could be built between a music of the object and a music of the note.

On the other hand, how can we fail to see that the road has already been embarked upon from the other direction? A musician with some experience of concrete music can, for example, recognize certain similarities in *Vodcek*. Messiaen is also a precursor using classical means, and not only because of his liking for musical matter, or because of his experiments in systematic structures in which the series is not entirely divorced from traditional language. Before concrete music placed the emphasis on the concept of the object, Messiaen was aware of it. If he finds inspiration in birds, it is not out of sentimentality or a desire to imitate them: the bird's song is his concrete experiment. This song has the double advantage of providing him with an object that is at the same time a language. Because birds are not human, their modulations provide schemas that are interesting in ways that are different from algebraic grids. The bird is a living being, part of a universe of muscles and nerves. Its algebra is organic, and so infinitely more complex than series of dry numbers, and yet it is simpler, and in any case more effective, because it is mysteriously linked to human sensibility.

I am going to give two examples of a way of working that seems to me infinitely more desirable than a priori mathematics and that will make my meaning clearer. We have talked a lot about the technical difficulties and the pure problems of musical structure. But is it altogether clear that these are the thorniest problems, or at least those for which we are the least prepared? Do we not experience the main difficulty when faced with the aim itself of music, particularly when the means become too numerous? Is music a language? Should a new branch of music turn toward the plastic Arts and get its inspiration from them? The example of the birds already showed that a musician who is seeking to escape from a solely anthropomorphic language can try to find his models in nature. But why not a holly leaf? Say a concrete musician comes into the studio with a holly leaf in his hand. He adopts it as his work template. The leaf has a distinctive color and shine. It has precise curves. It has one whole smooth lobe, and on the other some prickles, which in their variety represent infinitely subtle exercises on one theme. Now, the instruments of concrete music allow an exercise like this. While the "piece shaped like a pear" was only a joke, the "holly-shaped melody," the polyphony inspired by the bunch of holly, is not pie in the sky. It is an experiment that can be done.

So music is not a holly leaf, it's a language? Never mind. Let's record a spoken phrase, listen to it, distort it as much as necessary so that all that is left is the melody, the rhythm, and all verbal content is lost. Haven't we got an excellent schema for the composer? Isn't he bound to find melodic and rhythmic inflexions here that are very far from harmonic norms, but, because of the way they have been constructed, are in tune with human sensibility?

In other words, what holds us up in the new music is where to begin. We go abruptly from an intuitive structure to the need for an explicit one. Until today, the composer has sat down at his desk and literally not known

what he is doing. Abruptly, a series of numbers is suggested to him to restrict the choices that put him in such a great state of disarray. Fine, but
this doesn't resolve anything; it's a negative rule. He needs a positive one.
Where can it be found except in resemblance and imitation?

I have just been to see a very beautiful film in color by Fernand Léger, made in New York, in which the painter, giving his own commentary on his method, over and over again emphasizes the object (another
one!). Finally, he says, we have substituted the object for the subject (the
word "object," of course, with its painterly meaning). Then we see Léger
walking through the American countryside or in the streets of Manhat-
tan, gathering many an object in his hand or his gaze and redrawing it,
painting it in his own way, utterly free and utterly faithful. This is the
birth of the work and of Art. Everyone who has seen this film, even if he
doesn't really like Léger's work, cannot but be charmed by the way it is
done. It is true that Léger denies doing abstract painting. Doubtless he
would be more willing to call it concrete. But wouldn't a person have to
be very unthinking not to see immediately that abstract painting does
not have such very different beginnings?

Either abstract painting is nothing more than daubs or automatic
drawing, or it too is a more or less conscious, more or less willed imitation of schemas. Where can these schemas be found if not in the world?
And if we absolutely refuse the forms and colors of the external world
(and how, in truth, can we escape them?), what we cannot escape are inner structures that, whether we like it or not, are dictated to us as nerve
or muscle reflexes by a kinesthesia that is an inseparable part of us. Ultimately, what we must realize, along with Le Lionnais, is that there are
such nuclei of structures within man, which are projected by artists into
various fields of sensory representation.[1]

So, in every attempt at composition, there is good reason to separate
more and more the instrumental means from the guiding structures.
The less advanced the technique, the greater will be the reliance on the

---

1. Stricker was already saying in 1885: A subject retains within himself heard music,
something that is not nature's acoustic; he has an idea of melodies that does not come
from auditory images (S. Stricker, *Du langage et de la musique* [On language and music]).

instrumental means. A man discovering the violin will at first play open strings and will admire their sonority. His music will be informed by the instrument at hand. Similarly, military music is based on the bugle. As for the guiding structures, the less clearly perceived and felt they are, the more they will be replaced by a system, by arbitrary complication or simplification.

The very first concern—and this is indeed the most classic precept of the Conservatoires—should be "work on your technique." Where is the technique of concrete music? Is it at the instrumental level, or is it at the level of composition? Both, but initially it is much more at the level of music theory.

As long as a new music theory has not been clearly defined, and large numbers of musicians, of concrete music or otherwise, have not been able to become aware of it, all of these problems will remain impenetrable. Below we give some examples from a glossary of musical terms with the new meanings such a theory involves. For now, it is enough to say that the three classical *variables* of music, pitch, duration, and timbre, are at present insufficient to describe a more general music adequately. These are the three physical dimensions of sound. They coincide, more or less well, with the musical effect. But in the same way that, in organic chemistry, it is quite inadequate to analyze a chemical into oxygen, carbon, and hydrogen, whereas it is of value to see if it is made up of known "radicals," it is now essential, in music that is so organic, to understand a series of musical entities representing basic sound families, to which any sound can be allocated.

So, in addition to the three *dimensions* of music, there is good reason to highlight the three *planes* on which these dimensions operate, not in order to characterize an element of a work, such as melody or harmony, but to characterize a fragment of sound, considered as a fixed object, before it is used for possible variations or developments. These three planes, which will be defined in some detail below, are *tessitura, dynamic,* and *spectrum.*

Concrete instruments are made, essentially, to be able to operate on these three planes. The *phonogène* operates mainly in tessitura, filters mainly in spectrum, and we are expecting a new piece of equipment to enable us to give a sound any predetermined dynamic form. Thus the problem of obtaining any sound object, as predetermined in advance as is wanted, is in theory resolved. The problem of assembling the objects is also, in theory, resolved. We shall see how much we should mistrust this provisional solution. The only precise way to create music out of even the least complex of sound objects is in fact montage. So note by note, chord by chord, we replace playing an instrument with scissors and glue, still note by note, and with harmonic or contrapuntal mixing in which the brain plays the part previously given to muscles and nerves. Compose for the voice, for the pianist's hand, our fathers, and even more our grandfathers, used to say. This means not only that the performer made free use of his muscles, or more precisely the muscular and neural development acquired through his work, in his performance, but also that the composer reflected in his work what those muscles could do. So, in addition to inner structures from his own being, mind and body, there was a certain finality in the composition, which would again come up against the flesh and bone of a human being.

In concrete music, glue and scissors are simply a test of patience, where the intellect alone is involved. How prone to err the intelligence is, cut off from both an interior melody and an external projection of its melody in and through the muscles of others! And how we would love to rediscover somewhere that happy muscular difficulty, the safeguard of a well-crafted performance!

And so we would like to direct future technical research toward transforming the gesture in music. Is such a piece of equipment conceivable? Certainly. Is it essential? Is it viable? For my part, I believe that if it is necessary to provide musicians with a piece of equipment like this for them to rediscover the inspiration of muscles, because they are incapable of the intellectual gymnastics that would have done it for them, then it's a lot of trouble for nothing. So, meanwhile, let composers of concrete music strive, as Denis de Rougemont advises, to "think with their hands."

A spectator at the concert given at the *Empire* had thought that the operator at the desk was controlling the sound objects perceived by the audience with the movements of his hands. A happy delusion. As a result he was amazed that he could be present at the most spontaneous of musical creations. I soon disabused him by informing him that, indeed, the operator had so little effect on the way the sound was produced that I had thought of giving three-dimensionality to the music, because here, at least, the correspondence between gesture and sound could be immediately achieved. Three-dimensionality only resolved the difficulty by turning it round. More precisely, it resolves another, and adds a further, term to the series of parameters, and thus of unknowns, in the new music.

How, in fact, is three-dimensionality linked to concrete music? It is linked either at the outset, when this new music is conceived, or at the end, during the performance, with the sound projection of works of concrete music. Do I need to say that here, too, there is the possibility of confusion? Insofar as concrete sound objects involve the plastic, it is perhaps not enough to represent pitch, dynamic, and timbre in a recording that takes absolutely no account of the conditions of listening. In real-life listening, should or should not these recorded sounds correspond to real representations, perceived in the concert hall by the three dimensions of the ear? Should they, on the contrary, as in classical music, be presented in their pure state, aspatial, as it were, just as it is of no importance to us if the cellos are on the right and the wind instruments in the middle? In any case, even if these notions have to be associated, there is no doubt that, for studying and in their implications, they should be separated.

As for hoping for one or several pieces of equipment for making the sound object itself that could represent gesture as clearly as the relief desk, it is difficult to make any prediction. Everything in the development of modern techniques indicates the opposite tendency. A film has only apparent spontaneity. It is obtained only after endless patience, and strict and laborious coordination, which not only links hand to brain but also specialist to specialist, technician to artist, and chemist to interpreter. The concrete music film is nothing other than a cinema of sounds, and we know that three-dimensionality in the cinema is an additional, and not necessarily major, problem.

Meanwhile, we are reduced to constructing new works, either by following an instinct that takes much more account of instrumental contingencies than personal aspirations, or by applying experimental structures from which, as I have said, we must expect experiments rather than works. In these two areas, Pierre Henry's most recent experiments, for the most part composed after the *Second Journal*, should be noted. Two periods can be distinguished in Pierre Henry's development. One, which he is getting ready to leave, and in which he had arrived at a harmony, to my mind quite pleasing, between what can be done immediately with instruments and what can be done with inspiration. All the pieces that he has grouped together under the title *Microphone bien tempéré* (The well-tempered microphone) display an adequate mastery of sound matter, this time directed by a fairly clear will and with a plastic development that never fails to charm. A piece such as *Batterie fugace* (Fleeting percussion), various African *drums* broadcast with success several times on the radio and performed abroad, show that there is continuity between fields that have been divided since ancient times under the names of "melodic instruments" and "percussion." With means that were still crude, Pierre Henry managed to create percussion melodies or extremely delicate patterns of sound trajectories on the three previously mentioned planes of tessitura, dynamic, and spectrum.

Two recent experimental pieces display another tendency from which it would be wrong to draw any premature conclusions. One is by Pierre Henry, the other by Pierre Boulez, who in so doing confirms his entry into the career of concrete musician. Pierre Henry has given the title *Antiphonie* (Antiphon) to a work in three parts in which, in the first movement (the only one completed), he contrasts cells in continual variation with complex sounds in sound series of dissimilar matter, like two choirs. The work as a whole is treated in a systematically different way. The performance of this work, abrupt as it is, nonetheless shows a new aspect of concrete construction. It is impossible to judge until after a trial period, which initially is up to the authors themselves. They need time to be their own judges. In any case, there will be no more vague approximations or trial and error at the turntable: magnetic tape has come in centimeter by centimeter, with a rigor shown in the working diagram that served both as score and as plan for montage (fig. 22). Pierre Boulez's work starts from a single sound, taken from the zanzi. Pierre Boulez's intention is to

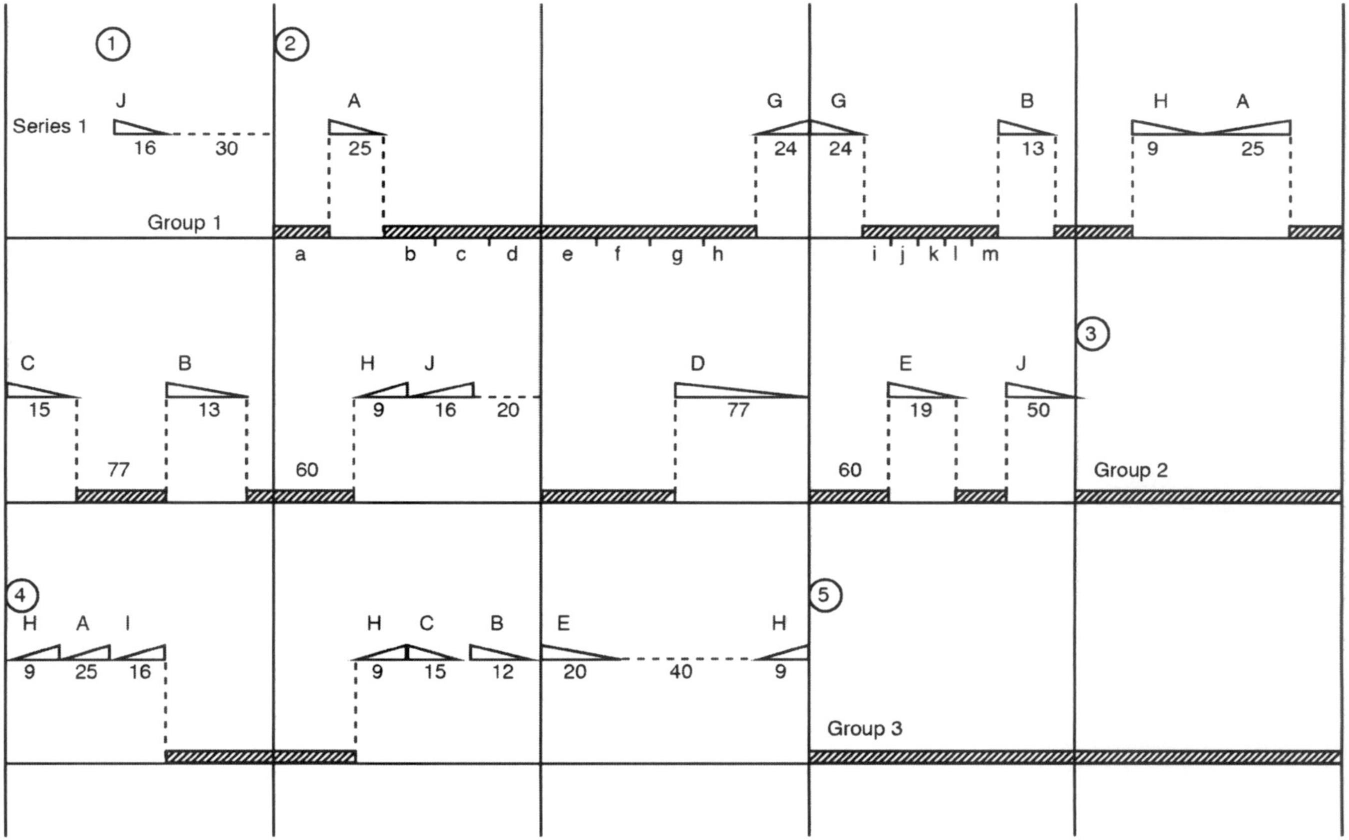
1
2
3
4
5
Series 1
Group 1
Group 2
Group 3
J
16
30
A
25
G
24
G
24
B
13
H
A
9
25
a
b
c
d
e
f
g
h
i
j
k
l
m
C
15
77
B
13
60
H
J
9
16
20
D
77
60
E
19
J
50
H
A
I
9
25
16
H
C
B
9
15
12
E
20
40
H
9

draw out systematic variations from this sound through acting on one of the parameters (fig. 23). So we have a study rather than a work. Nevertheless, this study is quite charming in its rhythmic language and the timbre melody it contains. The single sound, as can be seen, has been greatly differentiated to achieve an effect like this. Where the single sound fails is in harmonic or melodic diversity, which in any case was not one of the aims of this study.

So it would be quite wrong to think that concrete music is a school, with its own aesthetic. Various are the temperaments of the young authors who are interested in it, and who above share the need to wield the pioneer's spade. Doubtless, in order to grasp fully what is going on, and what has the best chance of going on into the future, it must be understood that concrete music will emerge through a series of violent transformations, which have their only possible parallel in painting, and this since impressionism. Whereas in painting this development has taken fifty years and has been staggered over several stages, it is likely that concrete music will bring in impressionism, cubism, realism, and surrealism all at once. It will be very difficult to keep track of ourselves. What, in fact, did impressionism contribute? The idea and the technique of fragmenting color, placing one brushstroke against another, putting color before form, and making form through color. Cubism introduced a breaking down into volumes. Impressionism and cubism do not for all that turn their backs on the subject; they continue to seek resemblance, or, at the very least, use the subject of a picture as a pretext to find interesting objects: forms and colors. A concrete musician would do

---

FIGURE 22 *(opposite)*. [Fragment of the score of *Antiphonie* (Pierre Henry).]

Antiphony: 2 parts alternating in opposition
①, ②, etc.: sequences
A–J complex notes from series 1: higher part
a–m segments of groups (▨▨▨▨): lower part
⬤➤: normal note
➤⬤: note backwards
- - - - - - : rests
16–30–25: duration in cm
unit of time at 60 cm: ♩

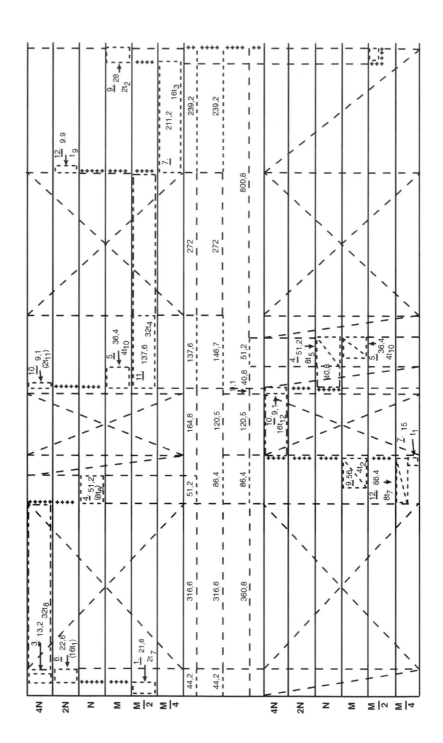

the same thing, not renouncing musical resemblance but using concrete means to fragment musical matter into new volumes (the complex note) or into new brushstrokes of colour *(Klangfarbenmelodie).* But it should be possible to recognize both a certain melody and a certain harmony in this technique, or at the very least a musical language that continues the former one. Others, on the contrary, believing that the subject (in the painterly sense) has had its day, will abandon it completely. The sound object, just like the visual object, freed from all need to resemble, is sought after for itself, is assembled in series or groups. Series and groups take the place of melodies and harmonies. This concrete music, which is the equivalent of abstract painting, deserves, like it, the name "abstract" much more than "concrete." The words don't really matter. And there again, there can be surrealism and realism, psychic or geometric climate. It's all this, somehow or other, that threatens (!) music through the unleashing of concrete musics, soon made to conflict with each other by authors as different—mutatis mutandis—as Manet or Braque, Dalí or Léger.

One thing is certain: we still do not know what will turn out to be possible. Not only technically, but humanly. In any case, a weighty past,

---

FIGURE 23 *(opposite).* [Fragment of the score of] *Etude sur un son* (Pierre Boulez).

This study is based on the interpolation of the transpositions of a sound in tessitura and duration. The entire keyboard is obtained, on the one hand, by producing twelve chromatic sounds on the *phonogène* from the initial sound, and on the other by multiplying or dividing the speed of playback, which gives six registers, multiples or submultiples of the normal speed N or half M = N/2 4N, 2N, N, M, M/2, M/4. The register 4N includes the twelve sounds notated t1, t2, etc. . . . In this way there is a sort of "tessitura" of tempi.

The study is then composed of series of sounds affected by durations calculated to form "parallel series," for example, when the sound t3 (4N) is affected by the duration value 32t, there is a silence notated by a series of dots.

The sounds are circled if they are played forward, marked with a diagonal if they are played backward.

The study comprises the concertante superimposition of two polyphonies.

a rich past, keeps us stuck for now with a one-dimensional music, for the dimension of pitch, as I've said often enough, dominates the West. Black music, or at least primitive black music, shows how, over millennia, rhythms and various percussion instruments can satisfy. Oriental music is unlike the first two because it has another side, a delicacy of touch, a quivering of sound bodies that is better than concerns about form. So we must understand, from such varied experiments, that there is a precedent, and a firm one, to the experiments in concrete music.[2] What appears difficult is to make the two extremes meet, to bring together such exacting techniques and ways from both a particular music of pitch, basically Western, and other musics, more complex yet less scholarly, prefigured, or merely suggested by other civilizations.

Insofar as the ear appears to be a sense particularly gifted at defining pitch, we can understand only too well the dominance of this parameter. Imagine that the eye could appreciate color within so many angstroms. There would doubtless be, alongside painting, a music of colors, with not only no form, but no *material medium*, a music of pure radiations.

And so Western music, as we have seen, is mainly concerned with the numerical values of pitched sounds. The experiment in concrete music reveals within the ear, and with almost no relationship to the musical ear, a sound eye, sensitive to the form and color of sounds, and also, as there are two ears as well as two eyes, to the three-dimensionality of these sounds. Imagine a perfect chord, made up of three notes, each one,

---

2. I would merely make a passing reference, but personally I attach great importance to the strange encounter between concrete music and so-called primitive musics. This is a good moment to recognize that extremes meet, and to explain why. On the one hand, the latest fashion in Western technique leads us to find sound objects that undeniably have more in common with exotic musics than any Western music. On the other, the aesthetic and psychological impressions produced by concrete music inevitably make us think about the role music plays in other civilizations. Finally, the concrete experiment in music allows us to approach the problems of exotic or primitive musics in a quite different spirit from Western musicologists. Unfortunately there was not enough time—and, even more, not enough competence—on the part of the author for these matters to be discussed here. I do not doubt that one day a study along these lines will tempt a specialist in exotic musics, who through personal experience of concrete music has found a method that can revitalize his understanding of other musics by allowing him to distance himself from Western music.

apart from a relatively pure basic sound, having weird forms and colors: one of these sounds is a pulsation, one a series of fluctuating attacks, the third an "aeolian" that seems not to come from the movement of any sound body. Moreover, the matter of these notes changes. Not only do they differ, but each of them develops. Finally, they scatter into space, tracing out trajectories there. In this example, in addition to the perfect chord these notes sustain, they cause sound forms and sound colors to appear and develop in time and space. Concrete music is nothing less than the bringing to consciousness of this phenomenon, until now implicit, and which no instrument had yet allowed us to grasp.

20 Farewells to Concrete Music

There is, between the faltering words of the first and second *Journal de la musique concrète* and the peremptory assertions of these latter chapters, a disparity that—quite justifiably—is bound to cause surprise.

Doubtless it would be convenient to interpret this as the disparity that always exists between our ideal and what we can achieve, between the elements that reality offers and the system that we would like to impose on them. There is also something else. These two very different parts of the same work are not altogether by the same author. One has worked with ingenuity, the other reflectively. One—or both—of them could be wrong, or both could be right. I am sufficiently aware to see that there are two planes, and to ask that others see this.

In reality, there is no reason why an inventor should be able to understand his invention, its impact and its potential. It could even be said that, generally speaking, the inventor is in the worst position to evaluate his discovery. Although he might be best placed to draw out its immediate applications, it is often left to his successors to tell which one really has a future. As for expecting an inventor to be able to work out the philosophy of his invention himself and to situate it in the context of his day, it is quite a strange anomaly that we should have already anticipated this.

Also, believe me, I do not claim to be that inventor who can see both sides; I am aiming for even higher, but in my opinion more acceptable, things: what I write about concrete music, I write in a different capacity, as if I were not the same man.

It is one thing to be in the studio, surrounded by machines and sounds. It is another to ask a machine to write down thoughts on concrete music. With the result that when I began to write, I was already no longer that man who invented equipment and manipulated sounds. I was inventing thoughts, manipulating words.

Finally, there is a third man, who ultimately is not at ease with any machine, whether for writing or singing. I am sorry to admit that, after having so loudly demanded that he work at one, this Luddite is the musician. But I am very much afraid that, although machines remain at a stage where we must either think too much or manipulate too much, the musician might not be on our side. With the result that, thirdly, I have had to turn myself into a musician.

A situation like this is extremely embarrassing and cannot continue for very long. One becomes weary of so much ambivalence and runs the risk of wearying others with ambiguity. Moreover, as long as one is being torn apart by two or three inner demons, each one, in a manner of speaking, preaching on behalf of his own saint, one cannot be an adequate force field. What is needed is a coming together of men who are less eccentric, in a sense more limited but more focused, who will each contribute more wholeheartedly a requirement, a competence, time. The ambiguous and the ambivalent can only play the part of precursors.

From the moment I was going to write and speak about this, I was implicitly making a choice. As an engineer, I would first and foremost have worked with machines, and there is plenty to work on for a long time to come. As a musician, I would have clung to my work with sound and not words. I would have been more attached to my works, even experimental; whereas the author before you makes little of his own works, if at least they have helped him, and will help others, to think. The case is closed.

By a curious paradox, until now concrete music has lived off fortunate misunderstandings; it undeniably brought about a rethinking of sound forms and matter; it was painters, sculptors, and poets who pricked up their ears and not specialists in musical sound. In any case, it demanded musicians abandon a priori thinking completely and return to experience. It was the dodecaphonists who first produced a contingent of volunteers. Laboratory experiments, still full of uncertainty, revolutionary certainly, and offensive to the ear: it was an Administration that encouraged anarchy, and it harbors the black flag.

For a person himself too divided, what a sorry success! While I dreamed of a rigorous classicism, new dimensions of the universe of the dominant, a harmony of the spheres, where man and God would speak the same language, there I was deep in matter, floundering in formlessness, surrounded by atonalists looking at me with cannibal eyes, and letting me live on in the hope that one day I would teach them to use a fork . . .

Five years of concrete music is fine for a musician if it leads to the future, to musicians, to music! But for a writer, it is time to stop, to step down.

I'm certainly not deserting, however. Two fields still require me: the field of means and the field of ends. It's farewell in the sense that I'm giving up writing music. Others are already taking up the gauntlet. And do not think that giving this up is not painful for me. But means doubtless have more need of my efforts. As for ends, I shall not be one of those who let go of new magic brooms without resisting if they are without responsible riders. This, at least, is my intention. Who at the present time can guarantee the future?

Where means are concerned, it is clear that at present we are following a radical course in music. The "most general possible" musical instruments, or at least their principles, have been found and are there in our studios as models. That these models are unsuitable for easy composing, and above all are inadequate for the enormous increase in *musi-*

cal potential that they entail, is a fact. But once we have said that these prototypes can modify both the matter and the form of a sound in every possible way, all that needs to be done is to "commute" these sounds in every desirable way. Doubtless, one day cybernetics will help to resolve this second problem.

Where ends are concerned, we need to know whether the end is man, or the fleeting success of some men. If success is a condition of duration, it is not impossible for the two ends to be pursued in parallel. If self-interest is the only motive for action in contemporary society, and profit the only criterion when Administration plays the part of Maecenas, we must, then, act out of self-interest and pursue a profitable Art. There is also a politics of scientific research, and a Machiavellianism of disinterestedness.

We must, indeed, understand that one of the particular characteristics of every new activity in our time is its collective nature. This will come as a surprise to musicians more than anyone, for, more than anyone, they still linger in august solitude. This will come as a surprise more in France than in Germany, and more in Germany than in America or the U.S.S.R. Atomic physicists do not each work at a desk, and their laboratories are more like factories than our traditional "labs." If, for music in the future, we talk about teams, like the teams of physicists around a cyclotron, we arouse sarcasm or indignation. But good heavens! Didn't music, long before all modern arts and techniques, give the example of collective discipline? What is an orchestra if not a cohort of fanatical individualists, but led by the baton? If the orchestra changes mode and is wholly replaced by sound reproduction, perhaps accompanied by cinematographic spatialization, we shall have to find it elsewhere. Progress on the contrary: all the musicians in this new orchestra will be composers. Much more than the previous ones, they create the work, are fully its makers.

The fact remains that experimentation does not stop there. On the contrary, it is only just beginning if we are concerned with making sounds accord with ears. If we allow that we have to be musicians to enjoy the classics fully, that we have to know our way around to appreciate jazz or exotic musics properly, then we must hope that the public will not expect to move into the domain of concrete music straightaway. It is because entering into it is so novel, and it so profoundly reshapes the phenomenon of communication or musical contemplation, that I thought it necessary to write this book. It urges the reader to take the steps required for any introduction: knowledge of the object, preparation of the subject. But the readership for which it is intended is not very great at the moment, nor is it composed of specialists. It should be a small fraction of the general public whom we have taken the trouble to prepare, a public that is experimental as well. It is to this public that these lines are addressed, and, even more, to those who will launch upon it the direct onslaught of their sounds.

PART IV Outline of a Concrete
Music Theory

In collaboration with André Moles,
Visiting Research Fellow at the
National Center for Scientific Research

I. TWENTY-FIVE INITIAL WORDS FOR A VOCABULARY

1. *Extract.* Any action producing a sound that is then recorded on a track of a disc or a tape is an extract. Extracts can therefore be either "live" sound recordings or sound recordings produced from preexisting recordings.

2. *Material classification of sound objects.* It is necessary to define a "material" classification of objects resulting from extraction before even submitting them to a technical or aesthetic analysis. This classification is based on the object's temporal duration and its center of interest, and it differentiates the sample, the fragment, and the element.

3. *Sample.* A sample is an extract of any duration (for example, from several seconds to a minute) that is not chosen for any well-defined center of interest.

4. *Fragment.* A fragment is a sound object of about one to several seconds in which a "center of interest" can be identified, providing it does not display development or repetition. If it displays these, the fragment should be limited to the portion that does not include any "redundancy."

5. *Elements.* If the analysis is taken even further, to the point of isolating one of the components of a sound object (a component that, furthermore, the ear can hear only with difficulty when it is isolated, and which in any case cannot be analyzed directly from sound), we say that the fragment has been broken down into elements. Examples of elements are an attack, a decay, and a piece from the continuation of a complex note.

6. *Musical classification of sound objects.* Once we have defined the "center of interest" that makes up the sound object, simply through limiting its duration, we must make a value judgment about its contents, whether it appears simpler or more complex. Thus we should be able to define the following: the monophony, the group, the cell, and the complex note.

7. *Monophony.* Cutting out in time does not allow us to separate out concomitant sounds. Only the ear can dissociate and separate these concomitant sounds into monophonic elements, which are then studied in themselves, through selective listening. Monophony in a superimposition of sounds is therefore the equivalent of a melody picked out by the ear from a polyphonic ensemble.

8. *Group.* A monophony of some length (a few seconds, or even some tens of seconds), studied for its repetitions or its inner development, is called a group.

9. *Cell.* By definition, a group is formed of either cells or complex notes. A cell is an ensemble with no repetition or development and does not have the definite characteristics of the complex note. Generally cells are dense complexes that develop rapidly (in rhythm, timbre, or tessitura) where even complex notes would be difficult to discern.

10. *Complex note.* Any element in a monophony that has a fairly clear beginning, continuation, and termination is called a complex note, by analogy with a musical note (which always has these simple characteristics).

11. *Large note.* A complex note can just as well be very short or quite long. A complex note is called a "large note" when its attack, continuation, or termination is sufficiently developed. If the development goes beyond a certain point, it will tend to become a group, and it will be possible to analyze its development in rhythm, timbre, and tessitura.

12. *Structures.* The totality of the material a composer chooses at the outset is given the name "structures." These may be cells or complex notes. They can also be ordinary notes, prepared or not, from unmediated, classical, exotic, or experimental instruments.

13. *Manipulations.* Any technique that changes structures before any attempt at composition is called a manipulation. Manipulations may be transmutations, transformations, or modulations.

14. *Transmutation.* Any manipulation that exerts its main effect on the matter of the structure without perceptibly altering its form is called a transmutation.

15. *Transformation.* Any manipulation that is intended to change the form of the structure rather than its matter is a transformation.

16. *Modulation.* If, without particularly aiming for a transmutation or a transformation, the intention is to selectively vary one of the parameters of a structure, or, more generally, if the intention is to develop the given sound in one of the three planes of reference of all areas of sound (tessituras, dynamic, and timbre), there will by definition be a modulation of the given sound, or the structure under consideration, in tessitura, dynamic, or timbre.

17. *Parameters that characterize a sound.* The parameters for variation of a sound can be understood either in the classical sense (there are three of them: pitch, intensity, and duration) or in the concrete sense (there are many more). It is preferable to use the concept of "plane of reference" rather than parameter. (See § II, III, and VIII.)

18. *Planes of reference.* The most complex sound phenomenon that can be imagined or encountered in practice ultimately comprises three planes of reference that can fully define it:

    1. *melodic plane or plane of tessituras* (the development of the parameter or parameters of pitch in duration) (see § VII)

    2. *dynamic or formal plane* (the development of the parameters of intensity in duration) (see § V)

    3. *harmonic plane or plane of timbres* (the reciprocal relationship between the parameters of intensity and pitch indicating the development of spectra) (see § VI)

19. *Performance procedures.* Performance procedures are all the procedures that, starting with given structures, and after the use of appropriate manipulations, make possible the performance of the desired work. There are three of these procedures: preparation, montage, and mixing.

20. *Preparation.* Preparation techniques (necessarily limited to the use of classical or paraclassical musical structures, i.e., notes that are more or less complex) consist in the use of classical or exotic or modern musical instruments as sources of suitable sounds without being particular about using them in the traditional way. Thus a piano can be an almost indefinite source of sounds, going from noise to musical sound, from pure percussion to continuous sound.

21. *Montage.* Montage techniques consist of assembling sound objects by simple juxtaposition, and in particular by gluing fragments of tape recordings end to end.

22. *Mixing.* Montage procedures do not allow polyphonic superimposition. Mixing, on the contrary, consists of superimposing compatible monophonies and recording the result.

23. *Spatial music.* The name "spatial music" is given to any music that is concerned with the localization of sound objects in space when works are being projected to an audience.

24. *Static spatialization.* Any projection that presents any monophony as if it were coming from an easily locatable source is considered static spatialization. This type of spatialization will consequently have been anticipated at the stage of mixing on synchronized but separate tapes, which are projected individually through separate sound sources, real or virtual.

25. *Cinematic spatialization.* The name "cinematic spatialization" is given to any projection that makes sound objects move in space at the same time as they move through time. This effect will therefore have been anticipated when the work was first planned; it is realized before an audience by a conductor-operator responsible for cinematic spatialization, with the help of appropriate equipment (spatial music projector, French patent no. 605467).

II. REVIEW OF ACOUSTIC CONCEPTS: THE THREE DIMENSIONS OF PURE SOUND

A sound signal can always be reduced to the combination of an appropriate number of elementary simple, or *pure*, sounds, which physicists call sinusoidal sounds (fig. 24), which are themselves defined according to their amplitude and frequency. The ear is not directly responsive to these two measures, but, according to a fundamental law of psycho-physics, it is responsive to their logarithm. We shall call the logarithm of frequency *pure sound pitch* and it will be measured in octaves—or their submultiples, *savarts*—and we shall call the logarithm of amplitude *level,* which will be measured in *decibels.* Thus a sinusoidal sound will be defined by its level, its pitch, and its duration, for no signal is of course unlimited, and the idea of a simple or complex *note* rests on the concept of duration.

Level, pitch, duration are the three *dimensions* of sound represented, in figure 25, by a line that shows the evolution of pitch and level in relation

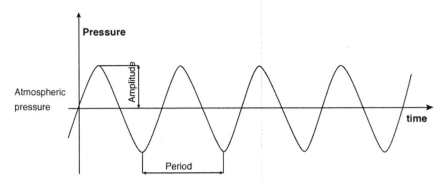

FIGURE 24. [Absolutely pure sound.]

to time: as the note has a finite duration, this line will have a corresponding length. Every complex note will be formed by combining these lines:
as each one of the simple sounds evolves within the time under consideration, some of them dying out, others appearing, all the lines together
will form a volume representing the evolution of the sound. As it is perfectly clear that a sound does not appear instantaneously but has a
continuous development from its initiation right up to its decay, this
volume will in general gradually increase from its basic plane and return
to it after some length of time. It is this volume that represents the *complex note*.

Thus, a piano note retains a number of components defined by their
frequency, and has a perceptibly constant relative proportion over its
whole duration, but its overall level will constantly vary in relation to
time, beginning with a rapid attack, then decaying very slowly. Figure
25 shows one of these notes with a constant timbre, and we shall call the
time-related curve in level the *form* of the sound.[1] Let us on the contrary
take the example of a noise such as the hissing of steam, starting suddenly: it will be characterized by the fact that it contains an almost
limitless number of components, with levels that vary completely arbitrarily across the whole acoustic range. It is a *statistical* sound, which

1. There is equipment (the logarithmic recorder) that gives the form of the note
straightaway.

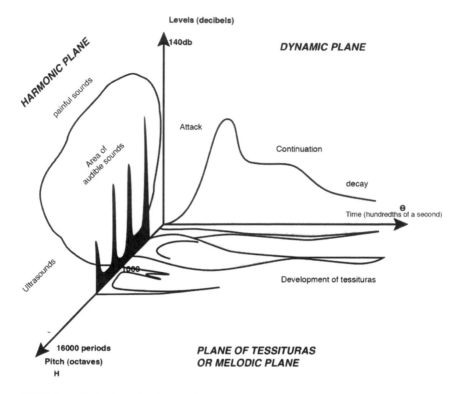

FIGURE 25. [Trihedron of reference.]

could go on indefinitely, but from its continuity we have cut an element
of duration—here quite arbitrary—that we shall call a *complex note.* In
this case it has a volume with a section that is very close to the whole
acoustic sphere, the sphere of audible sounds, shown in figure 26 and
remaining statistically constant throughout the duration under consideration. Through the use of technical procedures, it could be given a
more or less rapid *beginning,* a *continuation* with a perceptibly constant
level, and a very gradual *decay,* providing it with a form that is not so
very far removed from the musical note that we used in our previous
example. So the main difference between this noise and the note used
previously is that the musical sound possessed an *order* evident in a
continuity in the distribution of its components, which are perfectly

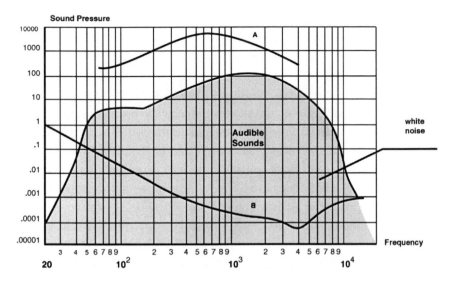

FIGURE 26. [Harmonic plane of a white noise.]

clearly defined. On the contrary, the noise of hissing steam has a huge number of components, in perfect disorder, and totally unpredictable. This is its essential characteristic, which, by analogy with optics, gives it the name *white noise*.

III.   GENERALIZATION OF THESE CONCEPTS
       IN CONCRETE MUSIC: THE THREE PLANES
       OF REFERENCE OF COMPLEX SOUND

In reality, no pure sound exists, either in Nature or in human art. Sound is called musical, in the classical sense, when a "fundamental" predominates enough for the name of a note, in the tessitura, to be given to it. In addition, this note has fluctuations that make this attribution more or less precise. On the other hand, such a sound is much more complex than most musicians imagine: it comprises not only accumulations of harmonics (and the way they are superimposed is not always stable, but varies in relation to the duration of the note), but also a large element of "noise." Over and above the musical sound, which is the most apparent in the whole sound phenomenon, a note on the piano, the violin, a vocal sound contains elements of noise, i.e., fairly complex "transitory phenomena," which there is no point for musicians to define, since they are all implied in the words "violin," "piano," or "voice" and are inherent in the sound of the instrument and the way it is used. Duration itself, which theorists believe they can manipulate precisely, is no more than an illusion. It is an abstract duration, allotted to the note. In reality, the production of any note does not take place in duration, as manuscript paper would have it. Every note has a beginning, establishes itself, then stops, all this in a great fluctuation of intensity, which gives the sound a *form*. And so the classical musician, because he does not have the power to modify or use them as a means of expression, ignores *implicit* musical parameters contained in the musical note that is reduced roughly to the three dimensions of pure sound. If we wanted to be not only more rigorous but nearer to the reality of music, instead of the three variables or parameters of the physicists, plagiarized by music theory (duration, intensity, pitch), we should use the concept of *planes of reference*, which emphasizes the development of the note itself, in addition to notes in relation to one another.

In other words, it is through an effort of abstraction and simplification—useful, it is true, and adequate until now—that we can speak of the three dimensions of musical sound and the development of a melody, for example, in duration (rhythm), intensity (nuances), and pitch (tessitura), complicated by the fact of harmonics (timbre), which are nevertheless *given* once and for all, as are the secondary phenomena (attacks, touch, vibrato etc. . . .) implicit either in the given instrument or in the performer under consideration.

If, independently of melodic development, we concentrate our attention more on the note, i.e., a single note from this melody, we notice that the phenomenon is not so simple. It may be true that, to the physicist, every sound, and particularly musical sound, can be *analyzed* and broken down into pure sound components, but an analysis like this is a further effort of abstraction, but which, this time, wholly bypasses the sense of hearing and no longer belongs to music, but to acoustics.

If we wish to delve any further into the phenomenon of music, using acoustic data only as a scientific base, and most definitely not as an aesthetic criterion (this is of the utmost importance), the concept of a parameter of melodic musical development must be enriched with parameters that characterize the musical note; and, even if they have a rigorous scientific justification, these new concepts must be accessible to the direct experience of the musical ear.

So, essentially, we must turn to the concept of *duration* and identify an external, or overall, duration that characterizes the note in the classical sense, such as its basic length, in relation to other notes in the melody, and its internal duration, where the passage of time is seen as the only possible indicator of the development of the note within itself.

It may appear surprising that such an important approach has not already been adopted by musicians, and that the need was only felt with the advent of concrete music. Even more, there can be no other explanation for the confusion felt by musicians, of concrete music or not, faced with the first experiments in concrete music than the lack of familiarity and aesthetic experience in this matter. If, for example, we imagine musical notes that resemble notes of a piano, violin, or voice, but in which the proportion of musical sound to noise is gradually inverted, we may easily think that classical music theory is losing its rights and is incapable of providing certainly values, and even an adequate vocabulary to characterize the new phenomena. These, already present in ordinary music, now become prominent.

In addition, wanting to make immediate aesthetic value judgments about the new music when one is incapable of defining, or even naming, the various occurrences of such phenomena is putting the cart before the horse, and wanting to write harmony before even having learned the theory of music. Hence the importance of the new concepts outlined here.

In particular the question "What instruments is this piece played on?" no longer has any meaning. The essential question is to be able to replace the word "instrument," which is widespread and convenient, and also an easy point of reference, with a sound-classification system, or sound characterology, which would enable sounds to be classified into families. Prior to, or together with, a theory, the characterology of sounds appears as the generalization of the concepts of instrument making.

There then arises the question of finding out where a characterology like this will come from. For a long time, musicians engaged with concrete music, wanting to avoid confusing acoustics and music, have attempted to do without the "trihedron of reference," which completely strips down every sound, however complex it may be, through three "projections" onto "planes of reference." Experience showed that it was practically impossible to do without these graphic representations, taken from acoustics. The combinations of sounds developed by the experiments of concrete music are indeed so multiform that a classification by comparison with a few basic types, defined empirically, has shown itself to be impossible.

So musicians have had to take on some of the concepts of acoustics, represented in Cartesian coordinates, on a three-plane projection of the cluster of curves, or even of volume, representing even the most complex sound phenomenon in a three-dimensional space. So the three classical parameters of pure sound into which musical sound was assimilated (duration, intensity, pitch) will be replaced by formal *characteristics*, distributed over three planes of reference by curves representing the development of the note, complex or otherwise. In other words, the classical parameters are considered to be stuck, at least in the broadest sense: the note in question has, generally speaking, a pitch, a duration, an intensity. If it is complex, it can have a whole "package" of pitches, an intensity that varies greatly in the course of its development, and a timbre that can be extremely complicated due to the interaction of fundamentals and harmonics modulated in various ways.

In conclusion, three numbers, representing values of the conventional musical note that are in general simple and arithmetical, are replaced by the three graphic representations of figure 25, representing the development—or, more precisely, the configuration—of the note itself. In some respects this method will give the molecular structure of the musical element.

IV. INDIVIDUAL STUDY OF THE THREE PLANES ENABLING THE COMPLEX NOTE TO BE REPRESENTED

From the definition that we have just given of the three dimensions of the complex note—level, pitch, and duration—we can, by adopting the methods of representation used in geometry, discern three *projections* obtained by combining the three preceding dimensions in pairs. Studying each of these projections will give us a way of understanding the note. We shall use the following terms:

- plane *of forms* or *dynamic* plane for the plane of development levels in relation to time
- plane *of spectra* or *harmonic* plane for the level-pitch plane
- plane *of tessituras* or *melodic* plane for the plane of variations of pitch in relation to time

V. DYNAMIC PLANE

The simplest of them, and the most scantily used in classical music, is the plane of levels in relation to durations or the dynamic plane. The curve representing the projection of the complex note in this plane, which we have called the form of the sound, generally begins at 0, if a complex note with an inner unity in the sense defined above has been isolated, for example by extraction from a closed groove or a tape loop. The note appears, then decays, the level returns to 0, and, generally speaking, we can discern three essential sections in its form:

- the *attack,* the onset of the note, often very abrupt in traditional instrument making (plucked strings, percussions, syllables)[2]
- the *continuation* of the note, during which it retains a perceptibly constant average level, despite some characteristic fluctuations (slow increase or decrease, vibrato, etc.)

2. We deliberately group together within the term "instrument making" all the technical resources of musical instruments, including the human voice, which is a very important instrument.

- the *decay,* the tail end of the note, the beginning of which is difficult to discern because it is not very different from the continuation but which in traditional instrument making is standardized due to the properties of resonating instruments, which give a very slow decay (mute, reverberation)

Concrete music, which is no longer limited by instrumental conditions such as these, will consistently use absolutely random note forms, and we shall give some examples of these, gradually moving away from the sounds of traditional music by relaxing the restrictive rules that arose from the nature of the instruments that limited it.

Attack of the Note

Thus, in the field of attacks, instrument making offered little more than three distinct modes:

a) *Plectrum*—or *plucked*—attack, in which a string was displaced from its initial position, then abruptly released. This is the steepest attack that can be found: the sound comes in immediately at its maximum level.

b) *Percussive* attack (piano): here a hammer hits a string, which vibrates after the time taken for the impulse to spread along the whole string. This attack is less violent than the preceding one, and it is also different from it mainly because the timbre produced is modified.

c) *Aeolian* attack (reed or violin bow), in which a string is made to vibrate very gradually, without any sort of discontinuity, for example by blowing a current of air across telegraph wire, or gradually making a violin string vibrate with a rosined bow. This is the same type of attack, even more gradual, as is made by the reeds of woodwind instruments (organ, harmonium).

Figure 27 a, b, c represents the form of the sound in these three basic examples.

Concrete music will liberate itself from these modes of attack, which we shall call *natural,* and replace them with more complex modes. Figure 27 d, e, f gives some examples of *artificial* modes of attack that we

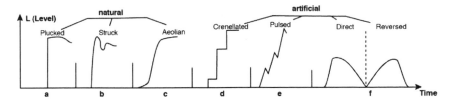

FIGURE 27. [Examples of natural or artificial attacks.]

shall be able to create, and which will supplement the previous ones. Better still, the techniques of concrete music will enable us to dissociate the characteristics of attack and timbre in familiar sounds.

Because of its practical importance we would draw attention to the mode of attack by *inversion* (27f), in which the forms of decay of the note are used systematically as the mode of attack: these forms are very progressive, for the decay of a natural sound is always a very slow phenomenon, and this is what gives music played backward its particular character. By simply adjusting the speed of decay, which can vary between several tenths of a second and several seconds, the whole character of the note will be changed without the general law of attack being altered. This single example shows how rich the contribution of concrete techniques can be in providing new notes or pseudoinstruments.

Finally, concrete music will use *impacts*, i.e., notes that in theory are reduced to *attacks*, with no prolongation of the decay through natural or artificial resonance.

Body of the Note

Here again, the physical rules that determine the functioning of traditional instruments have given only an extremely limited number of combinations: the simplest, of course, is the perfect consistency of the sound level (horizontal form), which seems as if it will go on indefinitely. Such is the case with a laboratory oscillator, for example. It is impossible to attain this indefinite consistency with an instrument controlled by a performer (violin, human voice). The hand trembles, the breath varies. Also, a device of the performer is a *vibrato,* which is generally an undulation of amplitude of about 10 to 15 percent, with five to eight undulations per second, and is used by all violinists and singers to conceal the inevitable fluctuations of their sound level. In this way it has gained acceptance in music and is perceived by the listener as an intrinsic characteristic of the note. Finally, the most apparent characteristic of the body of a note in theory is that it has a clearly defined level that the composer has become accustomed to marking on his score with symbols:

ppp   pp   p   mf   f   ff   fff

corresponding, according to Stokowski, to the following numerical values:

+ 20 decibels + 40db + 50db + 60db + 75db + 85db + 95db

Overall, the characteristics of the bodies we have just enumerated are very poor, and the simplest devices of concrete music technology will increase them considerably. For example, systematically increasing vibrato, which is impossible in traditionally made instruments because it would lead to unacceptable fluctuations in the pitch of notes, will give rise to so-called *pulsed* sounds, as in figure 28a. This concept will be generalized by also giving the name "pulsation" to every note obtained by rapid (usually artificial) repetition of the same impulse.

We use the term:

artificial, because it cannot be found in normal instruments, for the sound process with a very clear lowest point in the middle of the body of the note, followed by a rapid increase (fig. 28b).

For example, we shall use the term:

crenellated for the process with a sequence of independent resonances, where it can be seen that very large numbers of combinations can be made from these. This is a sequence of irregular maxima and minima (fig. 28d).

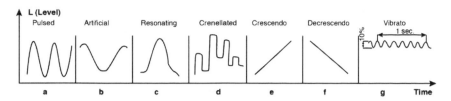

FIGURE 28. [Example of the allure of the body of a note.]

We shall use the term:

resonant for a sound characterized by a single increase in level in the middle of the body of the note (fig. 28c). This resonance can also be equalized artificially with the potentiometer.

rubbed, the process with a sustained action (reed or bow, for example) that gives an intermediary effect between the crenellation and the resonance (fig. 28g).

Finally, many complex notes will not have any definite shape; we shall simply describe their *crescendo* or *decrescendo* development (fig. 28e and f).

Decay of the Note

The decay of sound elements can be much better described in its form than its duration, for if it is quite easy to determine the instant when a sound completely disappears (when it is lost in background noise), it is still quite tricky to define the beginning of the decay, which is generally combined with the body of the note itself. In traditional instruments (violin, piano, voice, etc. . . .), it is a convention to call *period of decay* the moment when the note is no longer sustained, i.e., when energy is no longer being given to the vibrating body. So it gradually expends the energy it contained, as much through sound wave radiation as through inner agitation, and the general laws of acoustics lead to a gradual decline in accordance with a so-called *exponential* law, for which we will use the general term *reverberation,* and which will have a very variable duration—from several tenths of a second to several seconds. This term

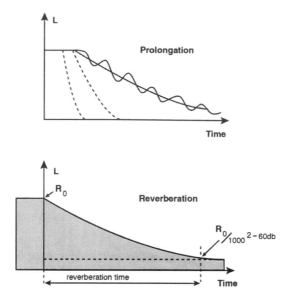

FIGURE 29. [Example of prolongation by natural or artificial reverberation.]

"reverberation" comes from the fact that most sound sources, after they have stopped vibrating themselves, radiate in the concert hall, which maintains the sound for a time, introducing a consistent *prolongation* to the listener's ear. In other words, in general the mode of decay of the concert hall replaces the mode of decay of the instrument itself; it is the former that is usually termed "reverberation."

In this large class of reverberating decays, or prolongations, we shall distinguish *continuous* reverberations, the simplest, and *vibrating* reverberations, which have the same characteristics of vibrato or impulse as the body of the note itself (fig. 29).

In traditional instrument making, the methodological distinction we have just made between attack, body, and decay of the note would be quite artificial, because traditional instrument making can give us only a very limited number of combinations of these various elements. So, for example, all the notes of the piano, attacked percussively, reach an instantaneous maximum, the body of the note is nonexistent, and the decay is very long, comprising only two numerical values, *pedal* or *muted*, which, considering their size, cannot really be modified by the concert hall. The violin note, and this is one of the causes of the richness, the success, and the difficulty of this instrument, has an aeolian type of attack, of very variable steepness (staccato, legato), a well-defined sustain with vibrato, and a fairly rapid decay, which is very subject to modifications from the concert hall.

Concrete music, on the contrary, will be able to dissociate each of these parts, choose its own character on aesthetic grounds, and assemble them, creating a considerable number of combinations, corresponding to an almost indefinite number of pseudoinstruments, and this on the dynamic plane alone, without even considering the planes of tessituras and harmony, which we shall now discuss.

VI. HARMONIC PLANE

The distribution of levels in accordance with the pitch of simple sinusoidal sounds that make up a complex sound, forms what physicists call the *spectrum;* amplitude in relation to frequency, or what musicians call *timbre,* which familiarity with musical instruments leads us to think of as stable within the note, and even as presenting a sort of sameness from one note to another, which leads us to speak of the general *timbre of an instrument.*

Strictly speaking, this concept of timbre will retain only momentary value in the complex note, since the level and pitch of each component develop independently over the duration of the note. In practice, however, various physiological and aesthetic reasons will lead the ear to cut out instants at least 1/20 of a second long from the continuity of the note, in which the spectrum of the note will be permanent enough to be considered as typical.

One of the most consistent characteristics of traditional musical instruments is the use of the vibratory properties of quite simple material bodies (strings, metal sheets, membranes, columns of air), which obey numerical laws, the main one being what is called the *harmonic law:* the frequencies of the various components of an instrumental note are simple multiples of each other or of a larger common divisor, the

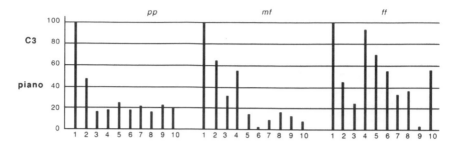

FIGURE 30. [Example of various harmonic resonances of a C3 on the piano struck at various intensities.]

fundamental, these frequencies being termed *harmonics* (fig. 30). Thus the spectrum of a musical instrument will present in the form of a certain number of harmonics—rarely more than about twenty—and their amplitude will generally decrease when the harmonic increase in frequency. Between these harmonics there is nothing: the musical instrument produces only a "discrete" sequence of simultaneous frequencies. The word *pitch* is used for the note given by the instrument, either the fundamental mentioned above, or the most important of the harmonics, and the indecision about this reflects the arbitrariness of this concept.

Outside the limitations imposed by traditional instruments, concrete music considers that every natural or artificial sound can, by reason of its position in a structure, take on a musical character, so it will seek to find a way of representing the immediate timbre of these sounds without turning to the quite arbitrary concept of harmonics. More precisely, we shall have to turn either to new concepts (thickness of sound), or to classical notions as far as timbre is concerned, depending on the extent to which a complex sound, composed of ordinary musical sounds, justifies these concepts, at least by analogy.

So first we shall have to discern whether or not a complex sound comes near to a musical sound, i.e., if it has a "spectrum of lines" or a "spectrum of bands."

The terms "thick" or "thin" will be used for a sound made up of a more or less extensive "package" of fundamentals (fig. 31b). Depending on the timbre of each of these fundamentals, it will be possible to classify the

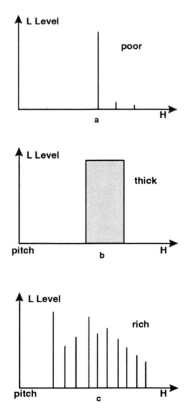

FIGURE 31. [Spectra of a sound that is: a, poor; b, thick; c, rich.]

resulting general timbre either quantitatively (poor or rich) or qualitatively (brilliant, bright, dark).

We shall use the terms:

poor, for a sound with a spectrum made up of only one or a very small number of components of significant amplitude (fig. 31a).

rich, for a sound that has a significant number of harmonics with significant amplitude. It is different from a thick sound in that it has a finite number of components that may be spread across the whole acoustic range instead of a continuous band in one piece (fig. 31c).

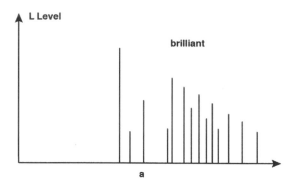

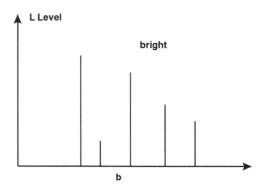

FIGURE 32. [Spectra of a sound that is: a, brilliant; b, bright.]

These quantitative characteristics of timbre will be complemented by the qualitative concept of *color*. We shall distinguish:

brilliant sounds, made up of a large number of harmonics, and where the amplitude does not decrease rapidly with the range (fig. 32a)

bright sounds, which have the same property, but with a very limited number of harmonics (fig. 32b)

dark sounds, which have only a few harmonics, and where the amplitude decreases rapidly with the range (fig. 31a)

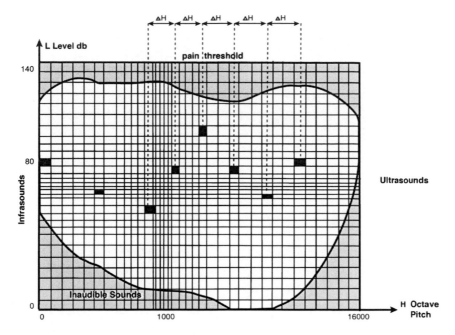

FIGURE 33. [Instantaneous spectrum of a complex sound in the course of development.]

This "instantaneous" spectrum is simply a cutting of the three-dimensional representation of a complex sound through a perpendicular plane on the axis of durations at a moment t.

VII.   PLANE OF TESSITURAS OR MELODIC PLANE

Strictly speaking, melodic development in relation to time, i.e., the development of the complete spectrum in duration, cannot be described in simple terms. However, the problem is simplified by a concept that is very important in the psychology of perception: *the thickness of the present*, a duration in which all acoustic phenomena are considered as simultaneous by the listener. This thickness of the present is of the order of 1/20 to 1/30 of a second: during this moment every acoustic element that appears—all the rectangles in the level-pitch spectral diagram (fig. 33)—are perceived simultaneously, and the section of the volume of the note

Instantaneous diagrams

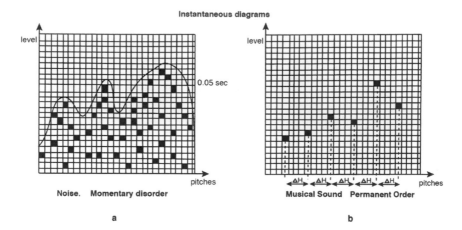

FIGURE 34. [Instantaneous spectrum: a, of a noise; b, of a musical sound.]

through the plane of tessituras, shown on this diagram, describes its melodic development over time.

In practice, the general laws of the theory of information in acoustics allow us to discern two types of very different moments in this development:

1) Very brief moments that in general correspond to periods of attack or very sudden change of form in the complex note on the dynamic plane. During these moments, the spectral diagram is very complex: a large number of rectangles is used simultaneously, forming what is usually called a continuous spectrum—white noise—and these elements have no simple numerical relationships to each other; they follow no or very few of the rules of selection set out in relation to the plane of timbres. They evolve haphazardly, in total disorder, during these short moments. Thus the concept of the transitory is linked to the concept of *noise*, or *disorder*, and this is quite a fundamental result as far as aesthetic perception is concerned (fig. 34a).

2) During the other moments, which constitute the major part of the duration of the complex note, and are separated into sections by the preceding moments, the spectral diagram is much simpler. With fewer elements being used, it develops slowly in duration,

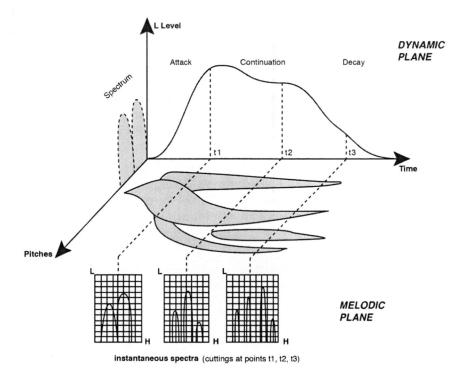

instantaneous spectra (cuttings at points t1, t2, t3)

FIGURE 35. [Instantaneous spectrum at the points t1, t2, t3 of a complex sound in the course of development.]

keeping a sort of memory, an approximate permanence, which gives the ear time fully to appreciate its modalities. An average tessitura can be distinguished here, with a perceptibly consistent spectrum (figs. 34b and 35).

So we shall distinguish the following tessituras:

a) *stable* or *unstable* depending on whether the average pitch over time is consistent or not

b) *rising* or *descending,* depending on the development of the average zone of the spectrum over time

c) *extensive* or *narrow* depending on the size of the musical interval (if it is discernable) in which they develop

At a more detailed level, we shall distinguish:

- *vibrating tessituras,* where the nominal pitch has periodic fluctuations, generally at a rhythm of five or six per second, with amplitudes of 1 to 5 percent in pitch, which furthermore correspond to the effects of vibrato already discussed under dynamic plane, to which they are linked by the properties of many instruments or pseudoinstruments: thus, a vibrato on a violin or an ocarina is always simultaneously a vibrato in amplitude and a vibrato in frequency

- *spun tessituras,* where the pitch of the complex sound develops very rapidly within a fairly limited margin during the course of the note, and especially toward the beginning and the end. This is an effect known in classical music with instruments such as the ukulele and the balalaika *(the Hawaiian effect),* or, to a lesser degree, the harpsichord or the zither

- *scintillating tessituras,* where the rapid connections between perceptible sounds, despite their disorder, does not allow them to be easily located

- *indistinct tessituras* (white noise)

VIII.   APPEARANCE OF CRITERIA FOR SOUND CHARACTEROLOGY

While keeping the word "parameter" for the variations of the classical note in duration, intensity, and pitch, we can define as *criteria* for characterizing sounds types of symbols used to analyze projections of complex sound on to the three planes of reference. In this way we can finally arrive at a method for classifying complex sounds into families.

We may also, out of curiosity, wonder how many types of sounds, i.e., ultimately how many pseudoinstruments, could be produced through *numerical combinations* of these criteria, by a generalization of musical means such as those at the disposal of concrete music.

On the other hand, we may observe that some of these criteria are not independent, that a certain criterion in the plane of tessituras automatically corresponds to a similar criterion in the dynamic plane. These will be *exclusions,* which will reduce the number of possible combinations.

Finally, we can look into certain families of particularly characteristic sounds that obey certain laws or set requirements. The necessary and sufficient conditions for obtaining such families, or at least for the possibility of obtaining them, will be the *conditions of compatibility*, by analogy with mathematical language.

We shall now develop these concepts one by one:

The main criteria of characterology, in the three planes of reference

The number of possible combinations (without taking exclusions into account)

Conditions of compatibility, in certain examples of particular interest

IX.   MAIN CRITERIA OF SOUND CHARACTEROLOGY (Fig. 36)

Total no. of criteria

A.   *Dynamic plane or plane of sound forms*

    1)   Criteria of attack   3

          The attack can be *plucked,*

                        percussive,

                        aeolian,

          depending on its steepness.

    2)   Criteria of sustainment, concerning the way the body

        of the note is sustained   6

          No sustainment at all; *impact*

          Sustainment by *natural* or *artificial resonance*

          Sustainment of the same type as the attack: *rubbed*

          Sustainment by repetition of the attack: *pulsation*

          Artificial sustainment by montage

    3)   Criteria characterizing the allure of the body of the note   5

          Stable (consistent intensity)

          Cyclic

          Continuous varied *(crescendo or decrescendo)*

          Discontinuous (crenellated, etc.)

    4)   Criteria for the decay of the note   5

          No reverberation *(muted)*

          Normal reverberation *(reverberating)*

          Artificial reverberation, which may in its turn have the

            preceding criteria *(continuous, discontinuous,*

            cyclical reverberation)

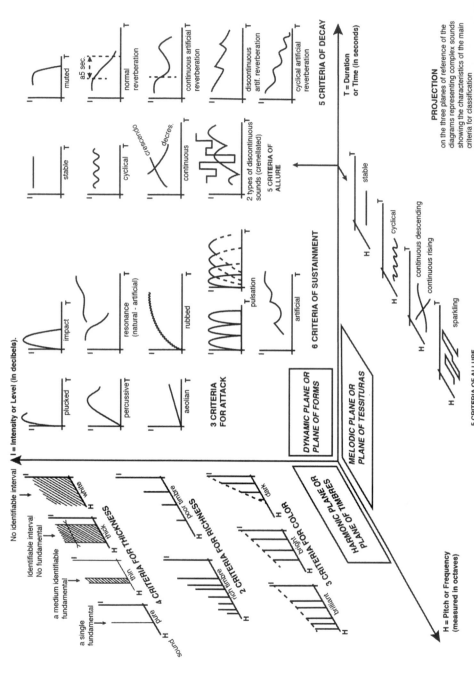

I = Intensity or Level (in decibels).

3 CRITERIA FOR ATTACK

plucked T

percussive T

aeolian T

impact T

resonance (natural - artificial)

rubbed T

6 CRITERIA OF SUSTAINMENT

pulsation

artificial

stable T

cyclical T

crescendo

decres.

continuous

2 types of discontinuous sounds (crenellated)

5 CRITERIA OF ALLURE

muted

a5 sec.

normal reverberation

continuous artificial T reverberation

discontinuous artif. reverberation

cyclical artificial reverberation

5 CRITERIA OF DECAY

T = Duration or Time (in seconds)

DYNAMIC PLANE OR PLANE OF FORMS

MELODIC PLANE OR PLANE OF TESSITURAS

HARMONIC PLANE OR PLANE OF TIMBRES

No identifiable interval

Identifiable interval No fundamental

a medium identifiable fundamental

a single fundamental

white

thick

thin

pure

sound

4 CRITERIA FOR THICKNESS

H

poor timbre

rich timbre

2 CRITERIA FOR RICHNESS

H

dark

bright timbre

brilliant

3 CRITERIA FOR COLOR

H

H = Pitch or Frequency (measured in octaves)

stable

cyclical

continuous descending

continuous rising

sparkling

5 CRITERIA OF ALLURE

PROJECTION

on the three planes of reference of the diagrams representing complex sounds showing the characteristics of the main criteria for classification

B.   *Harmonic plane or plane of timbres*
   1)   *Thickness of sound* (or purity)   4
       So-called *pure* sound (one single fundamental)
       Thin sound
       Thick sound
       White sound
   2)   Strength of timbre   2
       Poor timbre
       Rich timbre
   3)   Color of timbre   3
       Brilliant
       Bright
       Dark
C.   *Melodic plane or plane of tessituras*
   As in the case of the dynamic plane, this concerns the allure
   of the body of the note:
       Stable tessitura (fixed pitch)   5
       Cyclical (vibrato)
       Continuous (rising or *falling)*
       Discontinuous (scintillating)

No. of main parameters retained: 33

X.   THEORETICAL NUMBER OF SOUND FAMILIES

Thus we can allow about twenty criteria of form, about ten criteria of timbre, and four or five criteria of tessitura. These are, in effect, all the terms in italics in the above summary.

The total number of sounds, grouped into families and identifiable as if they were produced by distinct pseudoinstruments, is therefore, in theory, given by the total number of combinations of these criteria. In reality, it should be much bigger if the degree of importance of each of these criteria were taken into account, for example, if we decided to distinguish sounds that were more or less thick or thin, or attacks that were more or

---

FIGURE 36 *(opposite)*. [Summary table of the main sound characterology criteria defined in each of the planes of reference.]

less plucked or aeolian. On the understanding that, to focus our minds, we limit ourselves to an approximate, and very arbitrary, enumeration that gives a provisional idea of both the number and the degree of intensity of each criterion as set down, we can easily calculate the total number of combinations. This is in fact given by the classification into families of all possible sounds that have in common a criterion of attack, sustainment, or allure or decay (dynamic plane), or else a criterion of thickness, richness, or color (harmonic plane), or finally a criterion of allure in tessitura.

The number of these combinations equals:

$$3 \times 6 \times 5 \times 5 \times 4 \times 2 \times 3 \times 5 = 54{,}000$$

that is, about fifty thousand possible combinations.

(Clearly this number is significantly reduced when there are overlaps.)

It goes without saying that the first task of classification that must be done in concrete music is to distinguish from the fifty thousand or so possible sound families those few hundreds that on first sight seem to be the most common.

Two families, or more precisely two groups of families, in any case, are very important:

symmetrical sounds (musicians quite improperly say: nonreversible, whereas they are absolutely identical forwards and backwards)

homogeneous sounds, i.e., sounds that are identical to each other in time, and necessarily present as a closed loop, since they have neither attack nor decay

XI. CONDITIONS OF COMPATIBILITY

A sound is symmetrical if it is symmetrical in the three planes of reference (timbre, dynamic, and tessitura) at the same time.

A sound is homogeneous if it is homogeneous in the three planes of reference i.e., if its timbre, tessitura, and dynamic are constant throughout its duration, or throughout the duration of a certain portion of the sound, which will be a homogeneous fragment.

Homogeneous sounds have important applications in concrete music, where in particular they provide loops for new instruments called *phonogènes* (French patent no. 561. 539).

XII. APPLICATION OF CLASSIFICATION CRITERIA IN CONCRETE MUSIC

The classification of the elementary sound object and the complex note, based on spatial representation of level, pitch, and duration, which we have set out above, is fundamental. But while allowing the problem of characterization to be tackled in an intelligible form, this clearly has serious disadvantages, one of which is the multiplicity of aspects a note can have, a multiplicity that is difficult to grasp through a simple formula. Physical classification, which is done in parallel with this, and which does not come up against this obstacle, cannot really be used in practice except as a rough guide, where a precise numerical expression is required, i.e., for the technician of concrete music.

Generally speaking, in experimental practice and especially in artistic creation, we should be wary of aspects of phenomena that are too precise, not because they are inaccurate, but because they polarize the observer's mind and consequently tend to restrict his imaginative powers, an error that raises the hackles of every experimenter in concrete music. Therefore, numerical or descriptive classification should only be used to set up a more *formal,* direct and comprehensible, even if more superficial, classification using the vocabulary set defined above.

This objective classification seeks to define the essential *apparent features* of the complex note, which can be referred on an individual basis to any of the planes, and to any of the parameters we have discussed previously. So it will try to establish a list of priorities for the questions to be asked in the process of a descriptive definition, or, if you will, the order in which the relevant parameters should be considered. For these purposes, it will be based on perceptual appreciation, which will reintroduce the listener's consciousness as a fundamental element in the apprehension of musical forms.

In practice, we shall study the general characteristics of a sound in the following order:

- First, we shall see if the sound possesses any clear characteristic without bringing in the concept of plane of analysis: an artificial, reversed or dissymetrical sound, for example.

- Then we shall consider whether there are any characteristics that establish a correlation between the planes of analysis above: thus, the "vibrato" is a phenomenon that very frequently occurs simultaneously in the dynamic and the melodic plane.

- Only then, if the complex note being studied resists these attempts at immediate analysis, shall we systematically examine its characteristics in relation to the different planes, taking them in the order in which they draw our attention, or, failing this, in this order: plane of timbres, dynamic plane, plane of tessituras. In fact, it very frequently happens that a sound presents a clear dominant characteristic and the others are only working adjuncts in comparison.

- Only when very similar complex notes need to be differentiated will quantitative notations for each plane be introduced, which will, in any case, in every case enable us to achieve an objective classification, involving, it is true, a complexity that we could still well do without.

XIII. CLASSIFICATION TECHNIQUE

The above outline resolves the problem on the theoretical level, but practice naturally requires the application of these data. A composition of concrete music is ultimately an assembly of structures: complex notes or cells. So at the outset it will use a reserve of "concrete materials" in a repertoire of structures. In general, each of these elements will be in the form of a recording on a disc or tape, carrying a number referring to an index card with an intelligible description of its characteristics.

A concrete music laboratory therefore has, for the richness essential to both theoretical research and experimental works, the greatest possible number of sound structures from prior experimentation. As experimental discoveries come in unpredictable order, each of them will be card-indexed, with recordings in chronological order. They are a purely practical catalog.

As the card index is built up, an analysis of it should be made and kept up to date in order to make the connections necessary for the most interesting structures to be classified into families. It is without any doubt this analytical card index that will enable progress to be made in the understanding of the musical object.

Index of Names and Titles

Works are by Pierre Schaeffer unless otherwise indicated.

Lightning Source UK Ltd.
Milton Keynes UK
UKOW02f0025260915

259309UK00001B/70/P